NEW YORK WATER SUPPLY.

NEW AQUEDUCT.

1882.

Compliments of

Hubert O. Thompson,

NEW YORK WATER SUPPLY.

DEPARTMENT OF PUBLIC WORKS.

REPORT

OF

HUBERT O. THOMPSON, COMMISSIONER OF PUBLIC WORKS,

TO THE

HONORABLE WM. R. GRACE,

MAYOR OF THE CITY OF NEW YORK,

ON

Proposed New Aqueduct and Storage Reservoir for Additional Supply from Croton River,

WITH DETAILED REPORT OF

ISAAC NEWTON,

CHIEF ENGINEER OF THE CROTON AQUEDUCT,

AND

OPINIONS OF CONSULTING ENGINEERS.

NEW YORK, FEBRUARY, 1882.

DEPARTMENT OF PUBLIC WORKS.

DEPARTMENT OF PUBLIC WORKS,
COMMISSIONER'S OFFICE, NO. 31 CHAMBERS STREET,
NEW YORK, February 23, 1882.

Hon. WILLIAM R. GRACE, *Mayor:*

SIR—In the quarterly and annual report which I transmitted to you on the 13th instant, I stated that under the direction of Mr. Isaac Newton, Chief-Engineer of the Croton aqueduct, with the assistance of Mr. E. S. Chesbrough, as Consulting Engineer, careful investigations and surveys have been made during the past year, to ascertain the best method of securing an additional water supply for the city; that these investigations and surveys have led to a definite plan for a new aqueduct from the Croton river to the city, the outlines of which I briefly stated; that upon examination the plan has received the approval of Mr. John B. Jervis, the distinguished constructor of the Croton aqueduct, Mr. James B. Francis, President of the American Society of Civil Engineers, and that it was also examined and approved by Mr. Robert K. Martin, under whose direction a similar work, the Baltimore water-works tunnel, was recently successfully constructed. I have now the honor of transmitting to you Chief-Engineer Newton's report of the proposed plan, with the opinions and approval of the eminent engineers who have examined it in all its various features.

The facts and circumstances which have led to the immediate necessity of another aqueduct or conduit to bring a large additional supply of water to the city have been so often stated in previous reports of this Department, and they are so fully understood and appreciated by you, and I believe by the greater part of the people of this city, that they need no repetition here.

The only questions which remain open for discussion are, as to the source from which the supply should be obtained, and the means of collecting it and conveying it to the city.

I believe there is no difference of opinion among engineers and others who have given the subject attention and study, that in regard to geographical position, quality of water, and facility of means for conducting the water to the city, the Croton river and water-shed is the most desirable source of supply.

The only consideration which has led to the suggestion of other sources, is a supposition that the Croton water-shed cannot be relied upon to furnish enough water at all times for a new aqueduct of the required capacity.

Let it be shown that this supposition or fear is groundless, and there can be no hesitation in rejecting, for very obvious and potent reasons, the propositions of obtaining pure fresh water from the upper Hudson river, from Lakes George, Erie, Ontario, or Champlain, from the Passaic or Hackensack rivers in New Jersey, from the Housatonic river in Massachusetts, or Connecticut, or from the streams in Rockland and Orange counties.

The project of using the salt water which surrounds the city, as an auxiliary to the city's water supply, continues to be brought forward from time to time, by persons who have evidently not given the subject sufficient consideration. The objections to it are so apparent and conclusive, that engineers do not consider it worthy of serious consideration.

In view of the many questions, however, which are put to me by citizens, why we do not propose or make preparations to use salt water, I will briefly state the objections to it.

We have now 512 miles of iron pipes, with 5,427 stop-cocks, and 6,496 fire-hydrants, to distribute the Croton water in the streets of the city. To make the salt water of real service for the very limited purposes for which it can be used, it would be necessary to duplicate the greatest part of the distributing system, and to erect and maintain pumping machinery and stand pipes, at a total cost of probably not less than twelve to fifteen million dollars. Considering that less than five per cent. of the present water supply is used for extinguishing fires and for cleaning streets, the principal or almost exclusive uses to which salt water can be put, the cost of a salt-water system, as compared with any of the new projects for an additional fresh-water supply of ample proportions, is so enormous as to place it out of the question on that ground alone. But there are other serious objections to it. The fire underwriters say that salt water used in extinguishing fires would be likely to do as much damage to merchandise as the flames themselves. The rapid corrosion of iron pipes along the river-front, where they come in contact with salt water, shows that it would soon corrode the mains, stop-cocks, and hydrants, and, in the opinion of the Chief of the Fire Department, wear out the steam fire engines. For use on the streets it is so objectionable in a sanitary point of view, that several years ago the Board of Health prohibited and forbade street sprinkling with salt water.

An additional fresh-water supply will not only accomplish all that can be attained by utilizing salt water, but will meet the many other equally important objects of an adequate water system, for which salt water would be useless. The salt-water plan may, therefore, be dismissed without further reference.

The supposition or fear entertained by many that the Croton water-shed is not capable of furnishing a constant supply for a new and large aqueduct, shows an imperfect knowledge or misconception of the facts. Accurate observations and measurements of the rain-fall and of the quantity of water running over the Croton dam for the past sixteen years, prove that in the driest of these years, 1880, the average daily flow of the Croton river was 250,000,000 gallons. All that is needed to secure that supply every day in the year is sufficient storage capacity.

The capacity of the Croton water-shed to furnish a mininum supply of 250,000,000 gallons per day being proven, the whole question is narrowed down to the selection of the plans and means to secure sufficient storage and to conduct the water to the city.

Chief-Engineer Newton's plan covers both the subject of storage, and that of a conduit from the Croton river to the city. In regard to storage it combines in the highest degree the merits of simplicity, efficiency and economy. Instead of constructing a number of smaller reservoirs on the slopes of the Croton water-shed, on sites established by surveys made under the direction of the Croton Aqueduct Board in 1857–58, it is proposed to build a dam on the Croton river at Quaker Bridge, about 4½ miles below the present dam, and 5 miles above the mouth of the river, forming a reservoir of 3,635 acres in area, with a storage capacity of about 32,000,000,000 gallons above the level of the proposed new aqueduct.

The advantages of this single reservoir as compared with a number of smaller ones in the upper portion of the water-shed are :

1st. It will receive the entire drainage of the 361 square miles of water-shed, including about 23 square miles below Croton lake, not included in any previous reports, plans, or calculations ; on the other hand, the combined drainage area of a sufficient number of smaller reservoirs on the sites heretofore selected, to contain 32,000,000,000 gallons available water, would be less than 200 square miles. Consequently the large reservoir would fill much more rapidly than the smaller ones.

2d. The estimated cost of building this reservoir is $4,000,000 being at the rate of $125 per one million gallons capacity.

The cost of building the smaller reservoirs was estimated by my predecessor, the Hon. Allan Campbell, in his report of August 12, 1879, at $200 per 1,000,000 gallons or $6,400,000 for a storage capacity equal to the large reservoir.

3d. Purity of water is better secured by large reservoirs than by smaller ones.

4th. By taking the proposed site the length of aqueduct required to convey the water to the city is shortened about ten miles, as compared with the plans proposed in 1875.

Though the dam is to be of unusual height, and will have to resist the weight of a very large body of water, the eminent and experienced engineers who have examined the entire plan pronounce it entirely practicable, as well as the best that can be adopted. Dams of nearly the same height have been successfully built and used in France and elsewhere.

The conduit from the dam at Quaker Bridge to the Harlem river at High Bridge, is to be a masonry aqueduct, circular in shape, twelve feet in diameter, and capable of delivering about 250,000,000 gallons of water per day. The Harlem river and Manhattan valley are to be crossed by syphons, and the remainder of the conduit between the Harlem river and the Central Park reservoir is to be in tunnel wherever possible. The distance from Quaker Bridge to the Harlem river, on the line selected, is 26½ miles, only 9-100 mile greater than an air line; it is ten miles shorter than the Sawmill river line, and 9½ miles shorter than the Bronx river line surveyed in 1875 under the direction of General Fitz John Porter. It has the further most valuable advantage of being almost wholly in rock tunnel, thus securing the greatest possible strength and stability of the structure, with the least cost for supervision and maintenance after it is completed.

The prominent features of the entire plan are:

1st. *Large capacity and facility for collecting and storing water.* The new reservoir will receive the entire drainage of the Croton water-shed, and hold 32,000,000,000 gallons of water above the level of the aqueduct, and can therefore supply 200,000,000 per day for 160 days without recourse to the flow of the river. With the 9,000,000,000 gallons of water in existing storage reservoirs and lakes, and 5,000,000,000 gallons in the new reservoir about to be built on the east branch of the Croton, the total available storage capacity will be 46,000,000,000 gallons, sufficient to supply 200,000,000 gallons per day for 230 days.

2d. *Large capacity and utmost attainable strength and security of the conduit to convey the water to the city.* The new aqueduct will be capable of delivering 250,000,000 gallons per day, the entire minimum drainage of the Croton water-sheds. This will supply a population of 2,500,000 at the rate of 100 gallons daily per capita, or 3,300,000 at the present rate of consumption (about 75 gallons daily per capita). Add to it the capacity of the present aqueduct, 100,000,000 gallons per day, and we can, if needed in the far distant future, convey to the city that amount of water from the Housatonic river, or any other proposed auxiliary to the Croton, and supply a population of 4,660,000 at the present rate of consumption.

3d. *Economy of first cost of construction, as well as subsequent supervision and maintenance.*

The cost of the new dam, reservoir, and aqueduct, as above described, including everything necessary to deliver the water into Central Park reservoir is estimated at $14,000,000 00

The cost of a new aqueduct of 150,000,000 gallons daily capacity by one of the two routes surveyed in 1875, with equal storage capacity as included in the new plan, and provision to deliver the water in the Central Park reservoir, is estimated as follows:

Sawmill river route.	$19,493,000 00
Bronx river route....................	20,119,000 00
Cost of new plan per 1,000,000 gallons of conduit capacity.	48,000 00
Cost of plans reported in 1875 per 1,000,000 gallons conduit capacity:	
Sawmill river route.....	103,946 00
Bronx river route.....	108,121 00

The substitution of one large reservoir in place of eight or ten smaller ones, distributed over the entire water-shed, and the construction of the shortest practicable conduit, with the greatest proportion of rock tunnel, will involve much less labor for supervision and maintenance of the works after completion than the works proposed under any other plan.

In conclusion, I can only repeat what I stated in my last quarterly report, that the character and reputation of the eminent engineers who have been engaged in the preparation and elaboration of this plan, and in its examination, is a guarantee that their conclusions give the best results which patient investigation, guided by professional ability, experience and judgment can secure.

Very respectfully,

HUBERT O. THOMPSON,
Commissioner of Public Works.

NEW YORK WATER SUPPLY.

Department of Public Works.

HUBERT O. THOMPSON, COMMISSIONER.

REPORT

OF

ISAAC NEWTON,

Chief Engineer of Croton Aqueduct,

ON PLANS PROPOSED FOR STORING AND CONVEYING AN ADDITIONAL WATER SUPPLY TO THE CITY.

OPINIONS OF THE CONSULTING ENGINEERS.

TABLES OF RAIN-FALL, ETC., ETC.

MAP SHOWING DRAINAGE AREA AND AQUEDUCT LINES.

NEW YORK:
MARTIN B. BROWN, PRINTER AND STATIONER,
49 AND 51 PARK PLACE.

1882.

TABLE OF CONTENTS.

NEW YORK WATER SUPPLY.

REPORT

TO

HUBERT O. THOMPSON,

Commissioner of Public Works,

BY

ISAAC NEWTON,

Chief Engineer, Croton Aqueduct.

CHIEF ENGINEER'S OFFICE,
NEW YORK, January 30, 1882.

Hon. H. O. THOMPSON,
Commissioner of Public Works:

SIR—I beg leave to present the following report of the result of the investigations and surveys made under my direction since my appointment as Chief Engineer, for a new aqueduct from the Croton river to New York. The surveys and maps previously made, together with other data on record, have been of great value, not only in the positive information they afford, but in the suggestions they have led to.

Surveys for an additional supply made since the construction of the present aqueduct, have been those of the Croton water-shed of 1857–58, and those made in 1875 under General F. J. Porter, for the Sawmill river and Bronx river plans. The description and estimates of the cost of construction for both these plans will be found in Appendix " A," attached to this report.

At the beginning of my study of the subject of bringing additional water to the City of New York, the various sources from which it has been proposed to obtain this supply were carefully looked into. These sources are the Croton, the Passaic, the Housatonic, and the Hudson and Hackensack rivers, and Lakes George, Erie, Ontario and Champlain, also the streams in Rockland and Orange counties. The use of wells and salt water to be raised into reservoirs by pumps for auxiliary supply was likewise considered.

All the sources, *i. e.*, from these rivers and lakes, with the exception of the Croton and Housatonic, were set aside as being out of the question on account of the immense cost, or uncertainty of sufficient supply; although some of them might be used as auxiliaries.

Since becoming satisfied that the Croton river is by far the most available and the most economical source of supply, I have simply endeavored to determine the best plan for storing and conveying the water of this river to the city.

The quality of the Croton as a pure and wholesome water, as well as the geological and other characteristics of the river basin are so well understood, that nothing on the subject need to be mentioned.*

The meteorological history of the water-shed of the Croton, as far back as there are any records, shows that with adequate storage capacity at the head of the aqueduct, an average daily supply of about 250,000,000 † of gallons can be relied upon in the driest years. The area of over 23 miles which will be added to the existing water-shed—*i. e.*, to the area shown on the water-shed maps of 1857-58—by the plan to be hereinafter described, would increase the average daily supply from 15,000,000 to 20,000,000 of gallons, thus making the total average daily supply of about 265,000,000 to 270,000,000 of United States gallons.‡

The following views have formed the basis of my investigations and have led to the conclusions arrived at :

1st. The Croton water-shed is adequate to furnish all the city will need for many years to come, provided adequate storage capacity is provided.

2d. The storage reservoirs must ultimately be of sufficient capacity to hold all, or nearly all the water of the Croton in the driest years,

---

* See Report, App. "A."

† See rain-fall and other tables in Appendix.

‡ The utmost safe capacity of present conduit is about 100,000,000.

so that none, or but very little, can waste over the dam. And eventually to carry over a portion of the surplus of wet years to supply the deficiency of dry ones.

3d. The nearer the storage reservoirs to the entrance of the aqueduct, if they are of sufficient capacity, the greater will be the quantity of water that can be gathered from the entire Croton basin, and the more rapidly will the reservoirs fill again after being drawn down. The time required to fill the existing storage reservoirs and lakes, after they have been drawn down, is a warning on this point which should be heeded. All the water which falls on that part of the basin situated below the several storage dam sites shown on the maps of 1857 and 1858, above what is necessary to supply the aqueduct, will run into the Hudson river over the waste-weir of the aqueduct dam, unless storage is provided at that point ; so without a reservoir at that locality, it will be impossible to secure storage in the dry years. Hence storage located at the entrance to the aqueduct is in the most advantageous position.

4th. The aqueduct capacity should be sufficient to convey all the water available from the Croton valley ; it should also be enough to convey a portion of the water from other sources of supply, which can be led into the Croton basin.

The capacity of an aqueduct 10 feet in diameter, with an inclination of 1 foot to the mile, is about 168,000,000 of gallons in 24 hours ; while the capacity of an aqueduct 12 feet in diameter, with the same inclination, is no less than 270,000,000 in the same time. The excess of cost of the 12 feet over the 10 feet conduit is believed to be of much less importance than the greater capacity obtained.

5th. The aqueduct as far as possible should be in tunnel, this construction being the safest, most durable, and the least exposed to malicious damage. The difference in the cost between tunneling and excavation, because of the improved appliances now available, has been greatly reduced since the Croton aqueduct was constructed ; and the saving in length of conduit which can be effected by tunneling over a construction on a line located on or near the surface of the ground, added to the decreased land damages, will probably make the former fully as economical even in first cost.

6th. Wherever it is necessary to cross depressions in the line, the aqueduct should be carried on masonry laid in mortar, or beneath the surface by syphons.

7th. Storage in the Croton basin is preferable to bringing water from the Housatonic for the purpose of providing against deficiency in the natural flow of the Croton.*

LOCATION OF NEW AQUEDUCT DAM.

It is evident this dam must be on one of three general sites: 1st. It may be above the present dam. 2d. The present dam may be used or another built immediately below it so as to raise the level of the Croton Lake. 3d. It may be on the river considerably below the existing Croton dam and embrace an additional drainage area to that which now supplies the city.

As to the first site, taking that chosen by the surveys of 1875 to be the most eligible for this locality. It is 5 68-100 miles above the entrance to the existing aqueduct. Here the topography of the country is such that it is not practicable to raise the dam sufficiently above the grade of the proposed aqueduct to make a reservoir which would store any considerable amount. A large area of country would be flooded merely to get water into the aqueduct, and large portions of this area would be shoal water.

The plans of 1875 contemplated a dam 30 feet higher than the present one, with no storage above the level required to keep the aqueduct full.

Those plans require 10.6 miles on Sawmill river route, and 13 98-100 miles on the Bronx to be in tunnel, and would increase the length of the aqueduct from its commencement on the Croton to the High Bridge 3 21-100 miles more than the present one, and nearly 10 miles more than the line located this year.

An aqueduct might be supplied from the level of the present lake, and about 1¾ miles above the present dam near Trout brook, and join the new line near the Pocantico river, making the length of conduit to High Bridge about 27¾ miles.

---

* Should the Croton basin ever prove inedequate to supply the city, it is possible that a supply may be obtained within the State of New York by crossing the Hudson by tunnel near Croton Point. When the time arrives this no doubt will be carefully examined before it is finally decided to construct conduits from other sources.

Take next the second site, near the present dam. It is regarded as impracticable to raise this dam, and the valley immediately below is not well adapted for another of much greater height. These plans moreover, would be inadequate without the construction of large storage reservoirs on the various branches of the Croton to secure a full supply of water for the aqueduct.

Take the third site; a considerable distance below the present dam. An examination of the Croton river below this point to the Hudson, pointed out an apparently favorable dam site near Quaker Bridge, about 4 50-100 miles below the Croton dam, provided a rock foundation could be found.

The geological characteristics of the valley and the sinking of pits led to making surveys for a dam at this place. The top water-line for the reservoir, or lake, as it would truly be, was run at 200 feet above mean tide, Croton grade. The present Croton lake is 166 17-100 feet above same datum. Calculations based upon these surveys show that the reservoir would contain over 32,000,000,000 of United States gallons of storage, above the level, necessary to supply an aqueduct capable of conveying about 250,000,000 per day to the city; or with a delivery of 200,000,000 per day (twice our present supply), the aqueduct would be supplied for 160 days without a gallon from the natural flow of the Croton. The existing storage in reservoirs and lakes is 9,000,000,000; the reservoir which will be begun in the spring, in order to place the full daily supply of 100,000,000, the full capacity of present aqueduct, beyond all doubt, and which is to contain about 5,000,000,000, would make the total storage nearly 46,000,000,000 of gallons; sufficient to keep up a daily supply of 200,000,000, for nearly 230 days without the natural flow of the Croton.

The great area, 3,635 acres, and great average depth of this new Croton lake would make it exceedingly valuable as a settling basin. The benefits of such a condition of the water supply can scarcely be overestimated, and hence the earnest efforts to take advantage of them.

The dam now proposed is a work that would have been considered, at the time of the construction of the present aqueduct, of too great magnitude to be undertaken. The remarkable progress of engineering since then makes such a structure the most advisable in this case. Successful works of the same character in France have given great satisfaction, and confirm fully the theories on this subject of Messrs. Montgolfier and Delocre, of France, and Professor Rankine, of England. The estimate of the cost of this dam, has been based upon no untried principles, but upon those so ably advocated by the eminent engineers above mentioned, and so signally justified by actual experience.

It may here be mentioned that stone dams of nearly this height have existed in Spain for a long time, and have been proposed elsewhere. In fact, we find, that as far back as 1835, a dam 150 feet high was proposed near the mouth of the Croton, for an aqueduct to supply this city. That dam, however, as far as the existing plans show, was entirely different in character from the one now recommended, not being in accordance with the principle so successfully carried out in France. Besides, it did not provide for any important amount of storage above the level of top water in the aqueduct; whereas, the great value of the one now recommended consists in storage capacity, sufficient to furnish 200,000,000 gallons daily for 160 days. Without this capacity it would probably be much cheaper to draw the city's supply from the present Croton lake.

AREA AND CAPACITY OF PROPOSED NEW CROTON LAKE NEAR QUAKER BRIDGE.

Elevation * above Mean Tide, Feet.	No. of Acres. †	Cubic Feet, Not Including Croton Lake.	U. S. Gallons, Not Including Croton Lake.
30	7	2,230,000	16,680,400
40	37	14,080,000	105,318,400
50	55	31,690,000	237,041,200
60	85	58,850,000	440,198,000
70	146	105,600,000	789,888,000
80	201	169,960,000	1,271,300,800
90	262	253,790,000	1,898,349,200
100	334	360,730,000	2,698,260,400
110	398	488,160,000	3,651,436,800
120	417	639,130,000	4,780,692,400
130	562	819,007,000	6,126,643,600
140	649	1,026,860,000	7,680,912,800
150	733	1,261,540,000	9,436,319,200
160	1,245	1,600,140,000	12,417,847,200
170	1,756	2,222,350,000	16,623,178,000
180	2,412	2,994,590,000	22,399,533,000
190	3,037	3,966,930,000	29,672,636,400
200	3,635	5,130,740,000	38,377,935,200

Your predecessor, the Hon. Allan Campbell, an engineer of large experience, and who gave great attention to the water supply in his report of August 12, 1879, referring to the storage reservoirs laid down on the water-shed maps of 1857, says: "It is estimated "that the average cost per million gallons of all reservoirs projected "in the Croton basin will be $200," and in the same report, referring to the storage capacity required for the proposed aqueduct

* Croton datum.

† The area of present Croton lake is included after the level of present dam is reached.

of 1875: "To supply another aqueduct with 150,000,000 daily, "also on the basis of the driest years, additional storage to the "amount of about 30,000,000,000 gallons must be provided," which would then make the cost of the necessary storage $6,000,000.

When it is remembered that the reservoirs projected in the Croton basin would flood for the most part fertile valleys, probably the best land in Putnam County, $200 per 1,000,000 gallons can hardly be considered too large an estimate for the total expense of all kinds necessary for impounding water. If a reservoir can be built on the site above pointed out and contain, as above stated, 32,000,000,000 of storage, the city can then afford to expend nearly $6,500,000 for such a work considered as a storage reservoir dam.

Owing to the sterile and rocky character of most of the land this reservoir will flood, as well as its vast dimensions as compared with the size of the dam, it is estimated as hereinafter stated that the total cost of the reservoir, including dam, will not be over $4,000,000.

But the storage it will contain is not the only advantage of a reservoir of this capacity, and located in this place.

1st. It saves nearly 10 miles in length of aqueduct over the location of dam made in 1875, and this saving would go far towards paying the whole cost of this reservoir.

2d. It is at the lowest end of the drainage of the Croton, and would collect water more rapidly and completely than other plans.

3d. It would add about 23 square miles to the area of the water-shed, equivalent to an average daily supply of from 15,000,000 to 20,000,000 of gallons.

4th. It would afford a settling basin of the grandest proportions; the loss would be much less from evaporation and other sources on account of greater average depth. It would avoid conveying the water through miles of rivers, brooks, and, in many cases swamps, before it reaches the aqueduct, while in very cold weather the supply from such sources might be wholly cut off by frost, as was the case (with the water from the storage reservoirs) in the winter of 1880–81.

The difference in the cost between a dam and land necessary to raise the water near Quaker bridge 142 feet above tide—which is the level necessary to fill the aqueduct—and what would be necessary to raise it 200 feet, is estimated to be about $2,000,000. Hence the cost of the storage for 32,000,000,000 would be about $60 per million of gallons, instead of $200, the cost per million by building on the sites far up in the Croton basin; or $2,000,000 instead of $6,400,000, for the same amount of storage, even if it could be collected in reservoirs higher up in the basin, as laid down on the Water-shed Map.

STORAGE.

The water-shed survey executed in 1857–58, as before stated, was made chiefly for the purpose of selecting the most available sites for storage reservoirs.

The following table contains a list of the sites then selected, together with other information of the utmost importance in studying this subject in order to reach a safe determination respecting the quantity of storage that can be secured in the Croton water shed by those reservoirs.

RESERVOIR SITES.

Table from Water-shed Map of 1857-58 of Croton Basin above the present Croton Aqueduct Dam.

RESERVOIR.	Area.	Capacity.	Drainage Area.	Extreme Depth of Dam.	Extreme Length of Dam.	Length of Reservoir.	Distance from Crot n Dam.	Elevation above Mean Tide.
	Acres.	Gallons.	Sq. Miles.	Feet.	Feet.	Feet.	Miles.	Feet.
A..........	485.00	5,211,015,625	20.45	64	1,500	12,300	9.500	390
B..........	192.00	1,701,835,337	15.2000	55	1,700	6,000	12.750	500
C..........	730.00	6,589,101,562	13.7100	43	1,700	16,600	14.300	550
D..........	1,008.00	9,033,632,812	41.9500	48	770	21,000	20.250	500
E..........	303.00	3,369,206,857	20.3700	64	700	7,500	23.750	600
F..........	600.75	6,120,335,937	12.5100	20.90	1,560	10,600	15.500	560
G..........	452.19	4,861,035,156	20.9045	73	541	12,200	18.700	375
H..........	384.67	2,490,062,500	75.4574	40	545	14,748	19.390	375
I..........	449.00	4,205,820,654	70.5230	62	331	12,745	20.447	415
J..........	191.38	2,314,074,703	11.9171	69	1,311	11,616	28.710	500
K..........	512.74	5,671,449,219	78.9000	72	904	14,809	15.215	275
L..........	262.75	2,328,217,733	26.8600	74	757	13,120	16.539	295
M..........	492.25	4,392,131,445	23.3449	72	925	12,300	13.831	316
N..........	197.00	1,676,049,171	30.9620	60	686	8,650	7.708	250
O..........	239.47	2,182,337,109	17.3170	90	1,170	7,629	9.970	305

Entire drainage area of Croton Basin, 338 82-100 square miles.

The total drainage area of all these reservoirs foots up 480.30 square miles, while the entire area of the Croton basin is 338.82 square miles; this is because the computed drainage of some of the reservoirs overlaps that of others, which shows that the Croton Aqueduct Board did not contemplate that all of these sites could be made available as reservoirs to the extent indicated by this table.

The drainage of some of them is so small that in a dry year they probably would not fill; for example, reservoir F, which has a drainage area of but 12 51-100 square miles with a capacity of 6,120,-000,000 gallons. An inspection of this map shows that if every one of these reservoirs were built they would not receive the drainage of over about 200 square miles, because they do not furnish storage for the waters of large areas for which reservoir sites have not been found. The total estimated capacity of these reservoirs is 62,000,000,000 of gallons; of this amount 8,230,000,000 is already secured by reservoirs E and G, which have been built, one at Boyd's Corners, the other on the middle branch of the Croton; this leaves 53,770,-000,000 as the remaining storage, assuming the drainage to be adequate to fill the reservoirs. It has been estimated that to supply another aqueduct on the basis of the driest years, with 150,000,000 daily, additional storage to the extent of about 30,000,000,000 must be provided; but as before stated, if all these reservoirs could be built they could only receive the drainage of about two-thirds of the Croton basin. The balance of the drainage above the quantity necessary to supply the conduits would find its way into the Hudson over the waste-weir of the dam, if not secured near the mouth of the Croton. It is extremely doubtful if even 30,000,000,000 gallons could be secured beyond all per-adventure by constructing storage reservoirs in the water-shed many miles above the entrance of the aqueduct. In short, the only way to secure the entire flow of the Croton in the driest years, is to have large storage capacity near the mouth of the river.

THE HOUSATONIC AS A FEEDER FOR NEW AQUEDUCT.

As stated in the quarterly report for August, 1879, surveys were made for diverting the waters of the Housatonic into the Croton water-shed as a feeder for a new and large aqueduct. The plan proposed for conveying this water to the Croton, in general terms, was mainly an open canal with a sectional area of 80 square feet, and an inclination of one foot to the mile, the calculated capacity being 100,000,000 gallons daily. The comparison of this plan of obtaining water for the new aqueduct with that of storage has been carefully studied in all its bearings.

The Housatonic is in Massachusetts and Connecticut, out of the authority of this State, which could, therefore, exercise no control over it, to prevent pollution, or enforce any regulations. The water would have to traverse about eighty miles with exposed surface before reaching the aqueduct, and in very cold weather there would be great danger of the supply being cut off or greatly diminished when the demand would be greatest.

This river is no doubt liable to the same fluctuations of volume as the Croton, and there is no probability that in a season of extreme drought 100,000,000 per day estimated could be obtained; but if it could, the damages to mill rights would doubtless swell the cost much beyond the estimate. It would be necessary not only to pay for all rights injured below the point of intake, but for preventing mill owners above from holding back water nights and Sundays during seasons of drought. The yield of the Croton basin averaged during August, 1878, 123,000,000 of gallons daily; in December, 1880, its average was but 33,000,000, showing a falling off of 73 per cent. This proportion applied to the Housatonic shows that it could not be relied upon to furnish more than 54,000,000 a day, because the available area of the Housatonic basin is only about double that of the Croton. If the lowest daily yield of the Croton be taken, now known to be only about 10,000,000, then the Housatonic could not be relied upon for more than about 20,000,000 daily.

The following table gives an estimate of storage required to supply conduits with 300 millions daily, supposing a year as dry as that of 1880, the driest yet known in the Croton Basin.

For May	3,797,500,000	gallons.
For June	5,962,500,000	"
For July	6,130,560,000	"
For August	6,200,000,000	"
For September	6,000,000,000	"
For October	6,200,000,000	"
For November	5,820,000,000	"
For December	6,147,000,000	"
Drawn from storage reservoirs	8,530,000,000	"
	54,787,560,000	gallons.

Existing storage ponds and reservoirs	$9,000,000,000
Quaker Bridge reservoir	32,000,000,000
Reservoir I, to be built	5,000,000,000
Still required	9,000,000,000
	55,000,000,000

If the difference in cost was in favor of the Housatonic plan, as compared with that of constructing storage reservoirs on the Croton, the disadvantages the former presents are so great as to be decisive against it.

HEAD OR LEVEL OF THE NEW SUPPLY IN NEW YORK CITY.

It is seen by the description of the Sawmill river and Bronx river plans, that the aqueduct proposed was to end near Jerome Park, 3 01-100 miles from High Bridge and 7 88-100 miles from the receiving reservoir in the Central Park. At Jerome Park there was to be constructed a receiving reservoir of 600,000,000 gallons capacity. The elevation of the new aqueduct at Jerome Park was to be 30 feet higher than the present one ; but a small proportion of this increased head would be available in the circulation on Manhattan Island, because the water was to be conveyed from Jerome Park reservoir to High Bridge and from thence under the Harlem river to the Central Park reservoir in cast iron pipes 48 inches in diameter.

If ten lines of pipes of this diameter were laid for this purpose it is calculated that the loss of head or pressure from friction alone would be about 20 feet, when the aqueduct is discharging its full capacity, by the time the water reached the south side of Harlem river. As the main discharge would be into the Central Park reservoir, the pressure at which water could be delivered from that source would not be increased.

The new works, wholly independent of the Croton, now being constructed, to convey the waters of the Bronx and Byram rivers will deliver water into reservoirs to be built at William's Bridge at an altitude of about 180 feet above tide, or about 50 feet higher than the present aqueduct, and the water which will be supplied from this source will suffice for the more elevated portions of the Twenty-third and Twenty-fourth Wards.*

No provision has been made in the Quaker Bridge plans for additional storage reservoirs within the city limits. The principal function of such reservoirs is to keep a supply in the city in case it is necessary to shut off the aqueduct. Hence the necessity for storage at this end will not be increased by building another aqueduct.

Any important change, with the view of raising the level of the top water-line of the Central Park reservoir, would involve great expense, and could not in any event materially diminish the high service area necessary to be supplied by pumping.

THE AQUEDUCT.

Several lines have been run in order to get the best location for an aqueduct, as far as possible in rock tunnel, from the Quaker Bridge reservoir to the High Bridge. A favorable line was found which measures 26½ miles to High Bridge, or only about 91-100 mile greater than an air line.

This line is remarkable for the comparatively small depth of the shafts necessary for constructing the tunnels, which is a matter of great importance, both with respect to the cost and time required to execute the work.

There would be required 33 shafts, averaging 101 feet in depth, between the entrance of the aqueduct and the High Bridge.

It is proposed to cross the Harlem river by a syphon, either tunnel through rock, or pipes laid on river bottom ; to cross Manhattan Valley by a similar syphon, and to build the rest of the aqueduct between the south side of Harlem and Central Park reservoir in tunnel wherever possible, the same as in Westchester County.

It is proposed to make the aqueduct a circle in sections lined with brick, 12 feet in diameter, and to have it leave Quaker Bridge reservoir of New Croton lake at the level of about 142 feet above tide, thus permitting 58 feet of storage to be drawn, and to discharge into the Central Park reservoir at 119 feet above the same datum.

	Acres.
* Area of Twenty-third and Twenty-fourth Wards, New York City................	12,317
Number of acres below 100 feet mean tide, Croton datum, to be supplied from aqueduct	8,352
Number of acres between 100 and 160 feet, to be supplied from Bronx.............	2,617
Number above 160 feet, to be supplied from Yonkers or by pumping...............	1,348

Such a conduit would have the capacity to deliver about 250,000,000 of United States gallons daily when filled to within a few inches of the top.

I need hardly call attention to the great advantages a conduit in tunnel presents over any other mode; such a construction would be as imperishable as any structure can be, and it is no small matter that it would be removed as far as possible from the danger of injury by evil-doers.

In preparing plans and making estimates for this conduit, I have had the invaluable aid of unrestricted access to all the plans and other data connected with the construction of the Baltimore aqueduct tunnel from Gunpowder Creek, kindly granted me by Robert K. Martin, the Chief-Engineer of the work. As this tunnel is in rock, and of the same size and character as the one herein proposed, we have a safe guide for estimates of cost. While the Croton tunnels are considerably longer in the aggregate than the Gunpowder (Baltimore) tunnel, they would have shafts of much less average depth and could consequently be worked more rapidly and advantageously.

TIME REQUIRED TO COMPLETE THE PROPOSED WORK.

The time required to construct the Baltimore tunnel may be taken as a guide in estimating the time necessary to complete the proposed Croton tunnels; as the drifts in the proposed work would be about the same length and through the same character of rock, while the shafts would be considerably less in depth, it can be executed in less time, other things being equal. Taking the most difficult section on the proposed line as the portion which would require the most time, and which would consequently govern the completion, it is estimated that the New York aqueduct can be constructed in three and a half years from time of commencement. It should be remembered that in tunnel construction the work would be carried on day and night, winter and summer.

It is more difficult to estimate the time which would be required to complete the dam; it would probably be found necessary to suspend the work during the winter, say from three to four months each year; but when this dam has reached the height of 135 feet above mean tide, or 119 feet above the ground, Croton datum, it can be made to supply the new conduit with about 100,000,000 gallons per day;

it is probable with a systematic prosecution of the work, it can be raised to this height in three and a half years, while a year and a half more would probably complete the work to the full height.*

The estimated cost of the proposed aqueduct from Quaker Bridge reservoir to the receiving reservoir in the Central Park is $10,000,000. As before stated, in making these estimates, I have had the aid of the experience gained in the construction of the Baltimore tunnel; the above estimate being based largely on that data, and on liberal prices for both labor and materials, it is believed that it may confidently be taken as the amount within which the work can be done.

The proposed dam would be constructed wholly of masonry; were it not for the contingencies which may arise in securing a proper foundation, a very close estimate could be made of its cost. This being the case, and with the knowledge of the ground obtained by over one hundred test pits and explorations with diamond drills, I have estimated an amount for the dam and reservoir hereinbefore described which should place it beyond contingencies. The estimate for the dam and reservoir is $4,000,000,† which, added to the estimate for the aqueduct, would make the cost of the new water supply $14,000,000. The details of these estimates are ready for your inspection.

I estimated early last summer that an aqueduct of 150,000,000 daily supply, with the necessary storage capacity, could be built for $12,000,000; subsequent examination has shown that such a work could be constructed for less than that amount. But increasing the size of conduit to convey 250,000,000 per day, instead of 150,000,000, the total cost was augmented somewhat over $2,000,000; the excess in cost was considered small to expend for an additional daily supply of 100,000,000 of gallons.

With such an aqueduct in use and with pipes already laid, it is safe to say that the head (or pressure) which existed when the Croton water was introduced would be again enjoyed, provided the waste does not exceed the present amount. It is expected that the Department will be able to diminish the waste.

* The Furens dam in France, 164 feet high, was completed its full height in four years.

† Should the dam owing to unexpected difficulties in the foundation cost one, or even three millions more than the estimate, the Quaker Bridge plan would still retain its decided superiority.

The following tables give the comparative cost and other particulars of the three plans mentioned in this report :

Table of Comparison of the Plans which have been proposed for an Aqueduct from the Croton Basin ; with Extension from High Bridge to Central Park Reservoir.

	QUAKER BRIDGE, 1881 PLAN.	SAWMILL RIVER. 1875 PLAN.	BRONX RIVER. 1875 PLAN.
1. Total length, miles....................	31.35	* 42.31	* 41.17
2. Capacity in million gallons daily.........	250	150	150
3. Total storage provided by plan in Croton basin, with dams just high enough to fill aqueduct, million gallons daily....	....	....	....
4. The same with dams, full height proposed, millions of gallons..................	32,000	....	....
5. Total cost including no provision for storage............................	† $12,000,000	‡ $13,093,414	‡ $13,719,529
6. Total cost including provision for 32,000,000,000 storage.................. ..	14,000,000	§ 19,493,414	§ 20,119,529
7. Cost of providing 32,000,000,000 gallons storage in Croton basin..............	2,000,000	6,400,000	6,400,000
8. Area of new lake including present Croton lake, acres	3,635	1,200	1,200

* From profiles.

† Estimate for aqueduct to High Bridge $10,000,000, for dam without storage $2,000,000 (see page 41) =$12,000,000.

‡ Estimate in Appendix "A" added to Mr. G. W. Birdsall's estimate (Appendix "B") for conveying the water to Central Park reservoir, by the plans contemplated in 1875.

§ The same as No. 5, with $6,400,000 for storage added.

Table of Comparison of the Plans which have been proposed for an Aqueduct from Croton Basin, terminating at High Bridge.

	QUAKER BRIDGE PLAN, 1881.	SAWMILL RIVER PLAN, 1875.	BRONX RIVER PLAN, 1875.
1. Total length from the Croton to High Bridge, miles......................	26.51	36.52	36.08
2. Capacity, U. S. gallons in 24 hours, millions..........................	250	150	150
3. Total cost with no additional storage.....	$10,000,000	* $9,191,989	* $9,818,104
4. Total cost with 32,000,000,000 additional storage in Croton basin..............	† 12,000,000	‡ 15,591,989	‡ 16,218,104
5. Cost per million of gallons of supply obtained, including 32,000,000,000 additional storage in Croton basin.......	48,000	103,946	108,121

* See estimate in Appendix "A."

† Estimating increase in height of dam for storage to be $2,000,000, see page 13.

‡ Adding cost of 32,000,000,000 storage at $200 per million.

A large amount of field and office work has been accomplished during the season, among other things, the flow-line of Quaker Bridge reservoir, 78 miles, and 21¾ miles of cross section lines have been run; over 100 miles have been run in Westchester County. A great deal of detail survey has been done to determine the proposed dam site, besides other surveys of a similar character; 78 borings to rock have been made in Harlem river above High Bridge. The data obtained from the U. S. Geodetic and Coast Survey has been a valuable aid in topographical work along the line of proposed aqueduct. We have had the advantage of the trigonometrical points and the detail surveys made under the late Professor Bache by the officers of the Coast Survey. Over 100 test pits have been put down on the proposed dam site, and two diamond drills are accomplishing good results in the bed of the Croton.

I have studied the entire subject with the aid of E. S. Chesbrough, Consulting Engineer. B. S. Church, Resident Engineer, from his long experience with the existing works has rendered valuable aid. The topographical work has been under the immediate charge of John Mechan, formerly of U. S. Coast Survey.

I am indebted to J. W. Adams for assistance in making up the estimates, as well as details of plans of aqueduct on which they were based.

Very respectfully submitted.

ISAAC NEWTON,
Chief Engineer.

NEW YORK, January 31, 1882.

ISAAC NEWTON, Esq.,
Chief Engineer Croton Aqueduct:

DEAR SIR—I concur with you in the views and recommendations of your report on the proposed additional supply of water for this city.

E. S. CHESBROUGH,
Consulting Engineer.

APPENDIX.

OPINION OF JOHN B. JERVIS, Esq., CONSTRUCTOR OF THE CROTON AQUEDUCT.*

ROME, N. Y., January 13, 1882.

To ISAAC NEWTON, Esq.,
Chief Engineer Croton Aqueduct, New York:

DEAR SIR—I acknowledged your favor of 10th December, 1881, also that of December 26, 1881. In the meantime I visited your office in New York, and obtained a knowledge of the general features of the plans and estimates of the proposed improvements for the supply of New York City with water. After full consultation with yourself and your Consulting Engineer, I now propose to reply to the questions you have propounded to me.

FIRST QUESTION.—*As to the Necessity of an Additional Supply of Water.*

As to this question, it does not appear necessary to go much into detail. For several years instead of adding to the supply as population increased, the over strained capacity of the present aqueduct has been the same, and no addition has been practicable to the supply needed for the largely increased population.

A serious failure in the present aqueduct, which has been a source of anxiety for several years, may arrest its functions.

New York has a very large shipping interest, that needs much water; since the introduction of the Croton, her manufactures have largely increased; she is reported now the largest manufacturing city in the United States.

The present population is too large to depend for its current supply of water on one aqueduct. Without further discussion of this

* Condensed by Mr. Jervis from his longer report.

question, I have no doubt that the important interests of the city demand an additional conduit.

SECOND QUESTION.—*Source of Supply.*

I noticed by the reports you gave me that surveys have been made, establishing the practicability of obtaining the supply from the Housatonic river in Massachusetts and Connecticut. Whatever feasibility there may be of drawing from this or any other source, it appears to me better that it should be held in reserve until the supply from the Croton valley is exhausted.

THIRD QUESTION.—*Position of Reservoirs for Storage—Importance of having them Large and well down the Stream.*

No doubt, large reservoirs are to be preferred and the nearer the lower end of the valley, the more effectual will they be to secure the whole drainage of the basin. The securing of large reservoir sites, instead of several small ones, is decidedly important in securing pure water. The high dam at the lower end of the valley certainly provides for the most efficient method of securing the entire drainage of the Croton valley.

FOURTH QUESTION.—*Practicability of a High Stone Dam—Its Safety—Precautions to be Observed; Means of Passing Flood Water during Construction of the Foundation—Height of Main Dam above Flow-line—Length of Waste-weir and Height of Water to be permitted above Flow-line during and after Greatest Storms.*

As to general practicability, I have no doubt; but it will be a high dam, so far as can now be judged, about 230 feet above rock bottom, or 180 feet above surface of ground. You may require to go lower to secure a rock foundation for the highest part; your soundings not being complete, I do not think you will have to go materially lower than now appears probable.

There will be no difficulty in making a wall of hydraulic masonry sufficient to sustain it against the power of the water above from overthrowing it.

The main question will be the power of the material to resist the crushing force of this weight.

I think you will have no difficulty in obtaining stone in the vicinity of the location that will sustain the pressure. Good brick will bear near four times the weight without crushing. I have no hesitation in expressing the opinion that the Ulster cement, with clean sand, will make mortar and concrete sufficient for this work. If you can find cement that is stronger, it will be prudent to use it in the lower section of the dam.

Means of Passing Floods during Construction.

The floods of the river will, no doubt, embarrass the work of construction, and as this will be a work of years, the precautions should be very efficient. Such a work cannot be executed without many contingent embarrassments, and you will find occasion for the most vigilant assiduity and your best professional judgment will be demanded.

The Height of Dam above Flow-line—Length of Waste-weir and Height above Flow in Floods.

The old dam has a waste-weir of 270 feet. In about 40 years since its construction, no flood has been reported except in one instance of a rise of 8 feet above the crest of the dam.

If I understand the location, and I have no doubt it was well explained to me, the facilities for a waste-weir in the proposed dam are very good. Its position will be in the subsidiary dam that is required north of the main dam, where the waste-weir and the channel from it will be in solid rock.

FIFTH QUESTION.—*Conduit in the Tunnel as much as possible, instead of an Embankment or in slight Excavations.*

There can be no question that a conduit in a tunnel through solid rock will be more safe, and require less repair than one on any kind of filling or in light cuttings.

In some cases the cost of filling in low grounds would be greater than that of tunnel in sound rock.

SIXTH QUESTION.—*Difference in Cost of Conduit of, say,* 150,000,000 *daily and one of, say,* 200,000,000 to 250,000,000 *not Equal to the Value of the Increased Capacity.*

It would require more calculations than I am now able to make, to determine what the difference of value may be. There is, however.

no doubt the large conduit will be less expensive, as compared to capacity, than the smaller one.

SEVENTH QUESTION.—*Level of Central Park Reservoir to be Maintained in New Works, but General Head throughout the City to be greatly improved by Additional Supply, probably without New Mains at first.*

The new aqueduct will greatly improve the facility for keeping full head in the city reservoirs, and consequently maintain more efficiency in the pressure on the distribution pipes. Whether an increase of the city mains may be found necessary, will depend on the experience of the effect of a full head in the reservoirs.

EIGHTH QUESTION.—*Danger to a City of the Importance and Magnitude of New York, of depending wholly on one Aqueduct.*

As to the propriety of a second aqueduct there can be no doubt.

Finally, I would say :

1st. The dam you propose, is practicable.

2d. That it is the best, and, in fact, the only plan that can secure the whole source of the Croton valley for the supply of its waters to the City of New York.

3d. Furnishing, as it does, a reservoir of large capacity, it provides a supply of water of the purest condition practicable.

4th. Though there will be more or less embarrassment from the floods of the river during construction, there is no reason to doubt they may be successfully overcome by the engineering skill you will be able to exercise on this subject.

5th. As to line and plan of aqueduct you propose, I see nothing to suggest. Your view of this I regard as well taken.

When the dam is carried to the height of the gate chamber, you can occupy the new aqueduct, should it be ready. This you will see.

With sincere wishes for your success in the construction of this rather bold, but eminently important and, as I believe, quite practicable work, I submit this paper.

Very respectfully,

JOHN B. JERVIS,
Consulting Engineer.

OPINION OF JAMES B. FRANCIS, Esq., PRESIDENT OF AMERICAN SOCIETY OF CIVIL ENGINEERS.

Isaac Newton, Esq.,

Chief Engineer of Croton Aqueduct :

Dear Sir—In reply to your communication of the 10th instant, requesting my opinion of the advisability of obtaining an additional supply of water for the City of New York, by the plan you describe, I have to say that, in addition to the brief description in your communication, I have been informed verbally by yourself and Mr. E. S. Chesbrough more fully on the subject ; have read various printed reports and documents relating to the general subject of the water supply of the city ; examined the maps, plans, and profiles of proposed plans in your office, and have made a personal examination of the site of some of the proposed works.

From information gathered as above, I beg leave to offer the following remarks on the several parts of the plan described by you :

Ist. To go to the Croton watershed for the additional supply.

Every year there is a waste of water from the water-shed much greater than the quantity now supplied to the city.

This can be made available, to a great extent, by additional storage reservoirs of sufficient capacity.

The alternative is to divert a supply from the Housatonic river, by means of a canal and tunnel into the Croton valley, estimated to cost, with the damages to the mill property on the river, about $2,500,000.

The canal provided for in the estimate I consider quite insufficient to provide for the obstruction to the flow from ice. I should recommend it to be made of much greater depth than proposed, with walled sides, instead of earth slopes, for at least part of the depth. As the canal would be about 30 miles long, this would add largely to the cost. I also consider the estimate of damages to the mill property much too low.

The Housatonic river being in another State would be, as you suggest, a very serious objection.

Your estimate of the cost of sufficient storage on the Croton river is $4,000,000. The cost of the Housatonic plan, in my judgment, would not be very much less than this.

There being no great saving in cost, the want of jurisdiction, to my mind, points decidedly to the Croton water-shed as being the proper source of supply.

2d. "To build a masonry dam on the bed rock near Quaker "bridge on the Croton, about 4½ miles below the present dam, and "thereby raise the water level to 200 feet above tide."

3d. "This reservoir thus made, to contain about 32,000,000,000 "gallons of storage above the line which will keep water 11′ 5″ deep "in an aqueduct 12 feet diameter."

This dam would be nearly 200 feet high in the highest part, and would be a work of great magnitude, but I think entirely practicable, and as it would include a larger water-shed than reservoirs higher up the river, and create an available storage capacity of 32,000,000,000 of gallons at an estimated cost of $4,000,000, or at the rate of $125 * per million gallons, it would appear to be the most economical mode of obtaining storage in the Croton water-shed.

In the report of the Commissioner of Public Works for the quarter ending June 30, 1879, "it is estimated that the average cost per "million gallons, of all the reservoirs projected in the Croton basin, "will be $200."

A point to be considered in a reservoir of this elevation and magnitude, is the probable loss from percolation, elsewhere than at the dam; the geological formation appears to be very favorable in this respect, but I think there would be some loss. I should expect, however, that the additional water-shed, which would be obtained at the proposed site, over that at the site of the present dam, would fully compensate for this loss.

4th. "To run the aqueduct from the dam to High Bridge as far "as possible in tunnel, and to avoid embankments whenever "possible."

The experience with the present Croton aqueduct is so clearly and distinctly in favor of avoiding embankments, and constructing either

* This includes cost of dam to full height.

in tunnel or open cutting, that I do not see that anything more need be said on that point.

5th. "To cross the Harlem river by a syphon, either tunnel " through rock or pipes laid on river bottom; to cross Manhattan " valley by a similar syphon, and to build the rest of the aqueduct " between High Bridge and the Central Park reservoir in tunnel " wherever possible."

6th. "To raise the gate-house at the present dam to suit the new " water level, and to thoroughly strengthen the present aqueduct " between this and the new dam."

7th. "When the new aqueduct is completed to rebuild those " portions of the present structure on embankment where it has shown " signs of weakness."

I am not sufficiently familiar with the localities to express an opinion on all these points.

Crossing the Harlem river by a high bridge I think should be avoided if possible, as being too much exposed to injury. Either of the modes you suggest would be far better in this respect, and I have no doubt much less expensive.

The thorough repair of the present aqueduct as soon as the new one is in successful operation, is no more than ordinary prudence would require.

Comparing the several plans to which you have called my attention:

New aqueduct on the Sawmill river route with a new dam across the Croton river, one-quarter of a mile above the head of Croton lake; length from dam to High Bridge 36.52 miles, 10.06 miles being in tunnel; the supply to be derived from new reservoirs in the Croton basin:

Estimate of cost of conduit and pipe work..........	$8,700,000 00
Cost of 32,000,000,000 gallons of storage capacity at $200.	6,400,000 00
	$15,100,000 00

New aqueduct on the Sawmill river route with new dam as above; the supply to be derived from the Housatonic river:

Conduit and pipe work as above..................	$8,700,000 00
Estimate of cost of supply from the Housatonic, as per report of the Commissioner of Public Works for the quarter ending June 30, 1879, $2,500,000; as stated above I consider this too low, for the present purpose say..........................	$3,500,000 00
	$12,200,000 00

By the plan you propose, called the Quaker bridge plan, the estimate is as follows, the estimate for the conduit for comparison with the other plans, being for a capacity of 150,000,000 of gallons per day, the same as for the preceding, requiring a conduit of not more than ten feet diameter:

Dam and land damages for reservoir..............	$4,000,000 00
27 miles of conduit..............................	8,028,000 00
	$12,028,000 00

In view of the great objection of deriving the supply from a source not within the jurisdiction of the State of New York, I think the choice would lay between the two plans deriving the supply from the Croton water-shed.

By the above estimates the cost would be much less by the plan you propose than by the Sawmill river plan, and I see no advantage that the latter plan would have to compensate for its increased cost; of the three plans considered as above, I have no hesitation in recommending the Quaker bridge plan as being the most advisable one to adopt.

Very respectfully,

JAMES B. FRANCIS.

LOWELL, MASS., December 30, 1881.

OPINION OF ROBERT K. MARTIN, CHIEF ENGINEER (NEW) BALTIMORE WATER SUPPLY.

BALTIMORE WATER DEPARTMENT,
CHIEF ENGINEER'S OFFICE, CITY HALL,
December 30, 1881.

ISAAC NEWTON, Esq.,
Chief Engineer, Croton Aqueduct:

SIR—I had the honor to receive from you a communication, dated December 14, 1881, containing your conclusions upon an additional water supply for New York City.

Having examined the maps, plans, profiles, and reports relating to the matter, and after having made a personal inspection of the site of the proposed dam near Quaker bridge, and a careful study of the subject, I beg leave to present the following report:

By reference to a "table showing waste of water over the Croton dam," it will be seen that a large amount of water annually goes to waste in the Croton water-shed.

This waste, if stored, would be more than enough for your present wants, and will be sufficient in the future, for a largely increased consumption.

Again, the Croton water-shed is the nearest large supply to your point of delivery.

These facts influence me in saying that the most available source from which to obtain an additional water supply is the Croton water-shed.

In order to store the water of the Croton water-shed, you propose building a masonry dam on bed rock near Quaker bridge, 4½ miles below the present Croton dam, and thereby raise the water-level in the Croton basin to 200 feet above tide, which will give a storage capacity of about 32,000,000,000 gallons.

In my opinion a dam of such a height as you propose should be of masonry laid in hydraulic mortar, which, in the hands of competent engineers, I believe to be entirely practicable. My own views are fully sustained by the experience of French engineers, with similar dams, of nearly the same height.

You propose to build an aqueduct from the dam at Quaker bridge to High bridge, as far as possible in tunnel, and to avoid embankments wherever possible.

An aqueduct is the main artery of a water supply, and should be located where it will be safe and give the least trouble in the future.

In my opinion, the best location for an aqueduct is in tunnel, where practicable.

The form of an aqueduct that I would recommend should be circular, the diameter sufficient to preclude the possibility in the future of wishing that it had been larger.

Harlem river and Manhattan valley can be crossed either with a tunnel or by pipes, laid on the river bottom, or beneath the surface.

There can be no difficulty in the raising of the gate-house, at the present Croton dam, to suit the higher water-level, and also strengthen the present aqueduct between the present Croton dam and the proposed new dam.

After your new aqueduct is completed, you can rebuild those portions of the present aqueduct, or embankment, where it has shown signs of weakness.

I consider that no large city should be dependent on a single aqueduct for its water supply.

Your plan of constructing a large storage supply at Quaker bridge is preferable to the building of storage reservoirs in the upper Croton basin.

These storage reservoirs, in the upper Croton basin, can be availed of in the future, when the storage at Quaker bridge becomes inadequate. The Housatonic plan, as a source of supply in place of storage, has objections. It is located in an adjoining State, where it will be difficult to exercise control over pollutions, or enforce regulations.

Furnishing a city with pure water through an open canal, at all seasons of the year, and guarding every avenue of pollution along its line, is a serious problem.

Is it not possible that the Housatonic will be subjected to the same diminution of flow as the Croton during a drought, and may you not, eventually, have to resort to storage, to keep up this supply?

After a careful study of the whole subject, I feel confident that the plan recommended by you is not only advisable, but the proper one for an additional supply of water for New York City.

Respectfully submitted,

ROBERT K. MARTIN,
Chief Engineer.

"A."

REPORT ON SAW MILL RIVER AND BRONX RIVER PLANS.

DEPARTMENT OF PUBLIC WORKS,
ENGINEER'S OFFICE, CITY HALL,
NEW YORK CITY, January 3, 1876.

Hon. FITZ JOHN PORTER, *Commissioner of Public Works:*

SIR—In compliance with your instructions, two surveying parties were organized under Mr. Charles J. McAlpine and Mr. Horace Loomis, to ascertain the best route for another aqueduct between the Croton river and the Harlem river, at High bridge.

These parties were placed under the charge of Mr. Thomas A. Emmett, who for the last four years has had charge of the reservoirs in the Croton valley, and whose report of the surveys and the estimated cost of the new aqueduct is hereto annexed. A careful examination of the Croton river was made, showing the most favorable place for another dam was about a quarter of a mile above the head of the Croton lake and just below the mouth of the Muscoot river. It is at this point proposed to raise a dam 30 feet above the lip of the present dam, which will form a reservoir and settling basin covering about 800 acres, and will be about seven miles in length and hold about 1,180,000,000 gallons.

Surveys for the aqueduct were made across the divide to the head waters of the Bronx, and down that valley, and also further to the west to the Pocantico and Sawmill rivers.

The length of the aqueduct from the reservoir to the High bridge, on the Bronx river route, will be 36.08 miles, and by the Sawmill river route 36.52 miles.

The aqueduct will start from the Croton river with an elevation of thirty (30) feet above the present aqueduct, and descend on a grade of 12.67 inches per mile to the vicinity of Jerome Park, at which point the high grounds fall away so far as to render the continuance of the aqueduct of masonry expensive and objectionable.

It is here proposed to construct a reservoir, and from this point carry the water in cast-iron pipes. The water in the reservoir will stand forty-two (42) feet above that of the waters in the reservoirs in the Central Park.

The estimate is based on an aqueduct of sufficient capacity to carry 150,000,000 gallons per day, which, with the present aqueduct carrying 100,000,000 will give a daily supply of 250,000,000 gallons.

The drainage area of the Croton basin, above the Croton dam, is 338 square miles.

In the report of the Croton Aqueduct Board, made to the Common Council in 1863, they estimate the daily flow of the Croton river at 338,832,128 gallons.

Mr. Tracy, late Chief Engineer of the Croton Aqueduct, in his report in May, 1873, says: "For many years past the Department has kept a gauge of the daily quantity of water flowing over the Croton dam, in addition to that which is conveyed to the city by the aqueduct, and during the past ten years an average daily quantity of 340,000,000 gallons has run to waste over the dam, in addition to the quantity that was brought to the city."

Professor Chandler, President of the Board of Health, who has made the Croton a special study, says of it: "We have an available supply of 387,000,000 gallons." Of the purity of the Croton water, he says: "The character of the Croton water-shed is of a nature to "guarantee water of the best quality. Mountains and hills of Lau- "rentian gneiss receive the rain-fall, which is quickly absorbed and "filteredby the pure siliceous sands and gravels, to gush out in "numberless springs, feeding the brooks which bear the sparkling "waters to the ponds and reservoirs. From these flow the large "streams which by uniting form the Croton river. This is finally "expanded by the dam at the head of the aqueduct, into a broad, "deep lake, the fountain reservoir, or Croton lake, in which the "quiet waters deposit the finer sediments and thus undergo a final "purification before they are admitted to the aqueduct. Nowhere "along the streams can anything be found which can render the "waters impure. Rugged rocks or bright green pastures generally "border them. At certain seasons of the pear, as when the snows "melt in the spring, and the waters scour the still frozen earth, the "water is often discolored when it reaches the city, and alarmists "begin to discuss the danger to be apprehended from the poisons "and miasmata which are derived from the bogs and morasses of "Westchester County and Putnam County. But we have never "been able to trace any sickness whatever to such sources, and do "not believe that any unwholesome impurities ever occur in our "water. The purity of the Croton water is remarkable." *

The present aqueduct is now bringing into the city daily all the water that it can carry with safety, and it is necessary that steps be taken at once to bring in an additional supply.

The importance of a full supply is too great to be dependent upon one aqueduct, and another should be built entirely away from and independent of the present, that in case of accident to one the other may not be affected by it. It is now impossible to keep the water out of the present aqueduct sufficient time to make the thorough repairs to it that it requires. Had we another aqueduct, the water could be drawn from it for such time as may be necessary to thoroughly repair it, when it could be made fully as good as when the Croton water was first brought through it in 1842.

In order to keep the supply necessary for the city until another aqueduct is built, meters will be required on all places where extra water is used to stop the waste, and every effort made to stop the waste in private houses. By such exertions the demand may be kept down to the present supply until such a time as another aqueduct can be built. Work on the present aqueduct was commenced in the fall of 1837, and the water brought through it and let into the reservoirs at Eighty-sixth street, in July, 1842.

The present facilities for excavating rock with steam drills will expedite work, but it will not be safe to expect the completion of the work and passage of water through it in less than three years after the work shall be placed under contract.

The quantities of work in the estimate for the new aqueduct are full and the prices such as the work can be done for.

Very respectfully, your obedient servant,

JOHN C. CAMPBELL,

Chief Engineer.

---

* From Report of Croton Aqueduct Board, 1863.

DEPARTMENT OF PUPLIC WORKS,
ENGINEER'S OFFICE, CARMEL, PUTNAM COUNTY,
NEW YORK, December 20, 1875.

JOHN C. CAMPBELL, Esq., *Chief Engineer:*

SIR—I herewith submit a report of operations in the field (together with profile and estimates) of the engineering parties who have been engaged in making surveys for a new aqueduct from the Croton to the Harlem river. The map is not quite completed, but will be sent to you in a few days.

The first party, under the charge of Mr. Charles L. McAlpine, began work on the 20th of August, locating the site for a dam across the Croton river one-quarter of a mile above the head of Croton lake, and establishing a flow-line for a new lake or settling basin 30 feet higher than the lip of the present Croton dam. From the point where the dam was located a line was run down the east bank of the Croton lake on a descending grade of 0.020 per 100 feet, or 1 56-100 feet per mile, which grade was continued to the end of the line. Leaving Croton Lake at the mouth of the Kisco river, the line follows up that stream to the summit between it and the Bronx river, and down the Bronx to the end of the route. The length of this roûte to High Bridge is 36 8-100 miles, of which 13 98-100 miles is tunnel, 19 9-100 miles in open cuts and embankments, and 3 1-100 miles in cast-iron pipes to the High bridge over the Harlem river.

The second party, under the charge of Mr. Horace Loomis, began on the 6th of September, at a point on Mr. McAlpine's line on the north bank of Kisco river, near its mouth, and crossing that river continued down Croton lake to a small stream called Trout or Van Cortland brook, and followed it to the summit or head waters of the Pocantico river; following down that stream four and a half miles, and thence across to Sawmill river valley, which was followed for twelve and a quarter miles, thence crossing the ridge to the valley of Tibbet's brook. In the valley of Tibbet's brook the line runs about three miles alongside of the present aqueduct, varying in distance from fifty to one hundred feet to the east of it, and on ground from thirty to forty feet higher. From where it leaves the aqueduct the line runs west of Woodlawn Cemetery and thence on high ground to its junction with Mr. McAlpine's line. The length of this route from the dam at High bridge is 36 52-100 miles, of which 10 6-100 miles is tunnel, 23 45-100 miles is open cuts and embankments, and 3 1-100 miles in pipes.

For the lake above the dam two flow-lines were run, one of them thirty feet and the other twenty-five feet above the lip of Croton dam. The area of land covered by the upper flow-line will be 860 acres, and the capacity is estimated at 1,180,000,000 of gallons. The lower flow-line will cover an area of 614 acres, and will contain about 765,000,000 of gallons. The upper flow-line covers the track of the Lake Mahopac branch of the Harlem Railroad, from one to six feet in depth, for a distance of 1,300 feet, and the lower flow-line for a distance of 400 feet nearly touches the track, the deepest place being one foot. The water by the upper flow-line will also cover about four feet above the lower chord of the railroad bridge across the Croton river, the track being laid on the upper one.

Two points were examined for receiving reservoirs in the vicinity of Jerome Park, one containing 65 acres, with a capacity of about 600,000,000 of gallons, the other containing about 60 acres, with a capacity of about 550,000,000 of gallons.

In making these surveys the country has been carefully examined, and lines run through every gap or opening that was found between the Bronx river and Pocantico river and the Bronx river line, which runs from the summit along the head waters of Sawmill river to Unionville, is connected with the Sawmill river line a short distance below that place. In crossing Sprain Brook, on the Bronx river route, the estimate is for carrying the water across that valley in cast-iron pipes. The inside area of the proposed aqueduct is 75 32-100 feet.

Estimates are made on the Bronx river and Sawmill river routes as being the most direct and presenting the fewest obstacles to the construction of an aqueduct, and I think the estimates annexed to this report will fully cover the cost.

I am indebted to Messrs. McAlpine and Loomis, and the young men under them, for their careful and skillful prosecution of the surveys, and their promptness and dispatch in making up the estimates and profiles.

Respectfully submitted,

THOMAS A. EMMETT,

Assistant Engineer in Charge.

ESTIMATES ON SAW MILL AND BRONX RIVER PLANS ACCOMPANYING ABOVE REPORT.

Estimate for Lake and Dam at head of New Aqueduct.

860 acres of land, including buildings		$300,000 00
Clearing and grubbing		5,000 00
8,500 cubic yards of earth excavation, at 25c		2,125 00
24,000 " rock excavation, at $1.25		30,000 00
2,000 " tunnel cutting in rock, at $6		12,000 00
90,000 " embankment, at 50c		45,000 00
500 " concrete masonry, at $6		3,000 00
4,500 " rubble masonry, at $5		22,500 00
200 " brick masonry, at $12		2,400 00
2,000 " cut-stone masonry, at $25		50,000 00
Gate-houses, gates, screens, etc		30,000 00
Making new road, raising railroad bank, and bridge		30,000 00
		$532,025 00

Estimate for New Aqueduct on Saw Mill River route, from Dam to High Bridge 36 52-100 *miles, of which* 10 06-100 *miles is in Tunnel,* 23 45-100 *miles in Open Cut, etc., and* 3 01-100 *miles by Pipes.*

300 acres of land for right of way, at $500		$150,000 00
Clearing and grubbing		5,000 00
660,000 cubic yards of earth excavation, at 30c		198,000 00
130,000 " rock excavation, at $1.50		195,000 00
254,000 " tunnel cutting in rock, at $6		1,524,000 00
200,000 " embankment, at 30c		60,000 00
75,000 " foundation wall, at $2.25		168,750 00
65,000 " protection wall, at $2.25		146,250 00
41,000 " concrete masonry, at $6		246,000 00
253,400 " rubble masonry, at $6		1,520,400 00
130,300 " brick masonry, at $10		1,303,000 00
6,750 " hammer-dressed masonry, at $15		101,250 00
3 miles of new roads		30,000 00
		$5,645,650 00
3 01-100 miles of 48-inch pipes (six lines), at $132 per foot		2,097,850 00
Gate-house		30,000 00
Estimate of dam		532,025 00
60 acres of land, at $2,000 per acre	$120,000 00	
350,000 cubic yards of earth excavation, at 25c	87,500 00	
105,000 " rock excavation, at $1.25	131,250 00	
120,000 " embankment, at 30c	36,000 00	
12,000 " puddle, at $1	12,000 00	

6,000 cubic yards of slope wall, at $2	$12,000 00	
Gate-houses, gates, etc.	50,000 00	
		$448,750 00
		$8,754,275 00
Add for superintendence and contingencies		437,714 00
		$9,191,989 00

Estimate for New Aqueduct on Bronx River Route, from Dam to High Bridge, 36 08-100 *miles, of which* 13 98-100 *miles is in Tunnel,* 19 09100 *miles in Open Cuts, etc., and* 3 01-100 *miles by Pipes.*

300 acres of land for right of way, at $500	$150,000 00
Clearing and grubbing	5,000 00
350,000 cubic yards of earth excavation, at 30c	105,000 00
230,000 " rock excavation, $1.50	345,000 00
360,000 " tunnel cutting in rock, at $6	2,160,000 00
100,000 " embankment, at 30c	30,000 00
55,000 " foundation wall, at $2.25	123,750 00
50,000 " protection wall, at $2.25	112,500 00
28,000 " concrete masonry, at $6	168,000 00
203,400 " rubble masonry, at $6	1,220,400 00
113,300 " brick masonry, at $11	1,246,300 00
8,000 " hammer-dressed masonry, at $15	120,000 00
2 gate-houses, etc., at Sprain brook	40,000 00
18,000 lineal feet of 48-inch pipe, at $22	396,000 00
	$6,241,950 00
3 01-100 miles of 48-inch pipes (6 lines), at $132 per foot	2,097,850 00
Gate-house	30,000 00
Estimate of dam	532,025 00

Reservoir near Jerome Park.

60 acres of land, at $2,000 per acre	$120,000 00	
350,000 cubic yards of earth excavation, at 25c	87,500 00	
105,000 " rock excavation, at $1.25	131,250 00	
120,000 " embankment, at 30c	36,000 00	
12,000 " puddle, at $1	12,000 00	
6,000 " slope wall, at $2	12,000 00	
Gate-houses, gates, etc	50,000 00	
		448,750 00
		$9,350,575 00
Add for superintendence and contingencies		467,529 00
		$9,818,104 00

EXTRACT FROM REPORT OF THE CROTON AQUEDUCT BOARD, MADE JANUARY 5, 1863, TO THE COMMON COUNCIL.

With an aggregate annual precipitation of rain and snow of 42 inches vertical height, which is about the average for many years past, the quantity falling upon the Croton basin, tributary to our works, is equal to an average of 667,674,257 gallons per day.

Judging from experiments made in other localities, the physical and geological features of which, while resembling the Croton basin to some degree, are less favorable as a whole, the loss from evaporation, vegetation, and such absorption as does not subsequently reappear in springs, may be put down as equal to 14 inches vertical height of the total annual rain-fall. Make a further deduction equivalent to one-sixth of the entire annual rain-fall, to cover loss by evaporation and filtration from storage reservoirs, and we find that a quantity equal to an average of 338,832,128 gallons per day, would find its way to Croton dam and the inlet of our aqueduct.

Were it necessary to use the entire yield of the Croton basin, a great portion, if not the whole of this quantity, could, by a proper system of storage reservoirs, be saved and made available.

"B."

Estimate of Mr. G. W. Birdsall, First Assistant Engineer, for conveying water from termination of surveys of Saw-mill and Bronx river routes, north side of High Bridge, to Central Park Reservoirs.

Estimated Cost of Laying 10-48″ *Pipe from North End of High Bridge to Connections with Central Park Reservoirs.*

	Lineal Feet.		
From north end High Bridge, by Sedgwick and Ogden avenues, to McComb's Dam, 4,800 feet	48,000	....	....
Across Harlem river to One Hundred and Fifty-third street, 1,500 feet	15,000	....	....
McComb's Dam road and One Hundred and Fifty-third street, and Eighth avenue to North Gate-house, Central Park, 5 pipe, 16,000 feet	80,000	....	....
Seventh avenue and One Hundred and Fifty-third street to Fifth avenue and One Hundredth street and North Gate-house, Central Park, 5 pipe, 18,000 feet	90,000	....	....
Total lineal feet	233,000	... .	....
82,000 tons 48″ pipe delivered at dock, at $30.	......	$2,460,000 00	
350 tons specials and branches, at $75	......	26,250 00	
Stop-cocks, hydrants, etc	......	71,000 00	
Hauling and laying 235,000 ft. 48″ pipe, at $2.	......	470,000 00	
60,000 cubic yards rock excavation, at $2.50.	......	150,000 00	
235,000 " earth excavation, at 30 c.	.....	70,500 00	
290,000 " filling, at 10 c.	......	29,000 00	
80,000 square yards pavement to relay, at 25 c.	......	20,000 00	
Extra expense crossing Harlem river—			
6,000 cubic yards concrete, at $10	......	60,000 00	
30,000 " excavation, at $5	......	150,000 00	
Contingencies	......	40,000 00	$3,546,750 00
Add 10 per cent for engineering and contingencies	......	....	354,675 00
	......	....	$3,901,425 00

TABLE 1.

SHOWING WASTE OF WATER OVER CROTON DAM.

MONTHS.	1863.		1864.		1865.		1866.		1867.		1868.		1869.	
	Depth on Crest of Dam. Inches.	Average Daily Waste Per Month. Gallons.	Depth on Crest of Dam. Inches.	Average Daily Waste Per Month. Gallons.	Depth on Crest of Dam. Inches.	Average Daily Waste Per Month Gallons.	Depth on Crest of Dam. Inches.	Average Daily Waste Per Month. Gallons.	Depth on Crest of Dam. Inches.	Average Daily Waste Per Month. Gallons.	Depth on Crest of Dam. Inches.	Average Daily Waste Per Month. Gallons.	Depth on Crest of Dam. Inches.	Average Daily Waste Per Month. Gallons.
January	10.45	492,889,805	9.36	401,909,383	10.20	444,492,829	5.50	180,493,695	4.39	129,086,655	7.96	299,813,000	8.67	343,350,000
February	12.18	577,015,622	4.47	148,840,523	5.75	218,319,680	16.80	1,119,330,543	14.73	773,323,600	3.65	87,636,000	.....	....
March	11.79	593,521,536	7.10	260,810,911	14.81	790,830,624	9.77	406,809,297	12.00	551,322,898	13.70	675,234,000	16.48	847,972,500
April	11.50	522,240,315	7.70	293,170,821	8.97	358,022,600	10.03	420,795,777	9.93	417,567,753	16.33	867,997,000	12.26	568,492,500
May	9.16	397,367,737	8.84	354,266,997	11.65	562,581,688	9.97	390,692,555	13.48	670,816,408	17.87	995,175,000	10.51	461,325,000
June	1.29	23,549,244	2.92	84,015,412	7.60	278,039,658	9.70	402,344,929	14.60	785,413,290	12.26	567,487,000	5.41	170,250,000
July	3.66	130,131,046	....	....	2.74	80,784,000	2.96	90,730,852	6.94	256,829,196	4.24	116,122,000	1.48	24,337,500
August.	5.65	195,376,905	1.60	50,596,702	7.13	279,516,724	3.97	139,504,212	13.40	700,459,214	7.30	261,112,000	....	....
September	1.80	38,813,937	2.00	50,574,082	0.12	1,348,158	3.13	169,831,484	9.33	417,856,399	16.73	908,317,000	.....	....
October.	3.27	124,938,305	4.71	144,042,562	0.15	2,998,362	2.59	144,919,622	7.55	290,193,855	10.90	476,797,000	9.45	387,750,000
November.	8.03	322,179,348	8.87	359,551,272	5.62	189,968,266	12.20	591,115,654	9.27	359,947,474	13.96	693,150,000	8.10	300,000,000
December	9.90	427,651,960	8.06	316,223,620	8.35	355,310,165	10.96	499,294,183	7.71	298,024,947	3.85	104,250,000	11.19	496,875,000
Average daily waste in U. S. gallons per year.		320,472,980	....	205,333,524	.....	296,850,229	.....	379,655,150	.....	470,903,474	.....	504,424,000	.....	327,300,000

TABLE 1—(Continued).

SHOWING WASTE OF WATER OVER CROTON DAM.

MONTHS.	1870.		1871.		1872.		1873.		1874.		1875.	
	Depth on Crest of Dam. Inches.	Average Daily Waste Per Month. Gallons.	Depth on Crest of Dam. Inches.	Average Daily Waste Per Month. Gallons.	Depth on Crest of Dam. Inches.	Average Daily Waste Per Month. Gallons.	Depth on Crest of Dam. Inches.	Average Daily Waste Per Month. Gallons.	Depth on Crest of Dam. Inches.	Average Daily Waste Per Month. Gallons.	Depth on Crest of Dam. Inches.	Average Daily Waste Per Month. Gallons.
January	13.51	657,000,000	1.16	22,125,000	7.75	285,300,000	13.34	639,322,500	13.78	675,600,000	0.88	11,077,500
February	14.31	712,950,000	7.47	271,875,000	4.76	137,370,000	7.56	272,250,000	10.68	465,000,000	11.83	533,925,000
March.	12.19	557,550,000	12.40	585,000,000	5.50	170 872,500	12.09	550,950,000	10.76	472,500,000	10.10	419,250,000
April.........	14.64	739,050,000	8.20	307,500,000	11.36	517,500,000	20.50	1,229,820,000	12.45	583,000,000	16.45	888,000,000
May..........	7.14	255,000,000	7.85	292,500,000	4.96	147,750,000	20.88	1,375,000,000	10.84	478,500,000	6.80	231,525,000
June..........	2.83	60,600,000	5.57	172,500,000	4.94	147,375,000	0.72	8,550,000	3.41	82,500,000	0.70	8,550,000
July....... ..	0.82	9,000,000	2.42	51,750,000	1.16	20,775,000	.....	....	3.08	69,000,000	0.40	4,125,000
August........	0.80	9,000,000	2.49	52,350,000	5.25	159,375,000	1.36	21,000,000	1.99	37,485,000	15.07	771,750,000
September....	.....	....	1.76	30,825,000	4.86	142,500,000	0.35	3,150,000	0.55	4,725,000	2.93	67,500,000
October	0.108	750,000	7.31	234,000,000	4.40	126,000,000	4.44	120,000,000	1.99	37,425,000	0.23	1,650,000
November....	2.04	37,500,000	13.53	657,750,000	9.92	417,750,000	5.78	206,250,000	1.23	20,250,000	8.05	300,000,000
December	2.04	37,500,000	8.58	330,000,000	5.93	187,500,000	11.53	516,750,000	3.05	68,850,000	6.90	240,000,000
Average daily waste in U. S. gallons per year..........		256,325,000	.....	250,680,000	.....	205,005,000	....	403,582,000	.....	249,750,000	.....	289,777,000

TABLE 1—(Continued).

SHOWING WASTE OF WATER OVER CROTON DAM.

Months.	1876.		1877.		1878.		1879.		1880.		1881.	
	Depth on Crest of Dam. Inches.	Average Daily Waste Per Month. Gallons.	Depth on Crest of Dam. Inches.	Average Daily Waste Per Month. Gallons.	Depth on Crest of Dam. Inches.	Average Daily Waste Per Month. Gallons.	Depth on Crest of Dam. Inches.	Average Daily Waste Per Month Gallons.	Depth on Crest of Dam. Inches.	Average Daily Waste Per Month. Gallons.	Depth on Crest of Dam. Inches.	Average Daily Waste Per Month. Gallons.
January	5.74	179,100,000	2.40	51,750,000	9.50	387,967,500	5.54	171,000,000	9.90	418,500,000	1.80	30,850,000
February.....	12.62	593,250,000	6.11	199,200,000	13.11	628,500,000	9.40	382,500,000	11.04	483,750,000	11.97	547,500,000
March	18.34	1,035,000,000	19.65	1,155,900,000	13.08	620,925,000	13.74	675,000,000	10.79	472,500,000	17.58	973,175,000
April.........	17.56	975,000,000	10.71	472,500,000	6.70	232,320,000	16.16	862,500,000	8.10	300,750,000	7.03	245,320,000
May	7.50	272,175,000	2.77	61,350,000	5.99	194,700,000	7.40	268,500,000	2.89	67,500,000	5.14	149,000,000
June	1.63	25,500,000	1.00	13,245,000	5.53	171,000,000	2.80	60,000,000	0.21	1,650,000	6.16	199,400,000
July..........	0.17	900,000	.....	....	1.37	22,650,000	1.40	22,500,000	0.30	2,400,000	0.48	4,925,000
August.......	.....	....	.....	....	1.39	22,875,000	4.00	105,975,000	.....	....	.....	....
September....	.....	....	.....	....	6.81	245,250,000	3.93	105,000,000	.....	....	.....	....
October	.....	....	2.50	52,372,500	2.47	52,350,000	1.51	24,375,000	.....	....	.....	....
November....	1.80	30,825,000	13.68	672,225,000	6.87	246,000,000	2.60	54,000,000	0.63	6,000,000	0.13	918,000
December	0.03	187,500	7.05	245,400,000	20 03	1,185,135,000	7.54	272,250,000	0.23	1,687,500	5.97	194,500,000
Average daily waste in U. S. gallons per year..........		259,327,000	.....	243,661,000	....	334,140,000	.....	250,300,000	.....	146,233,000	.....	195,465,600

NOTE.—As the flow over a dam does not vary directly as the depth of water on it, and the averages being made from single daily measurements, the above table is not *absolutely* accurate, but as close an approximation as is required.

TABLE 2.

AVERAGE DEPTH IN AQUEDUCT AND AVERAGE DELIVERY IN GALLONS PER DAY.

Months.	1868.		1869.		1870.		1871.		1872.		1873.		1874.	
	Depth in Aqueduct at Sing Sing.	Delivery of Aqueduct.	Depth in Aqueduct at Sing Sing.	Delivery of Aqueduct.	Depth in Aqueduct at Sing Sing.	Delivery of Aqueduct.	Depth in Aqueduct at Sing Sing.	Delivery of Aqueduct.	Depth in Aqueduct at Sing Sing.	Delivery of Aqueduct.	Depth in Aqueduct at Sing Sing.	Delivery of Aqueduct.	Depth in Aqueduct at Sing Sing.	Delivery of Aqueduct.
	Feet.	Gallons.	Feet.	Gallons.	Feet.	Gallons.	Feet.	Gallons.	Feet.	Gallons.	Feet.	Gallons.	Feet.	Gallons.
January	....	....	....	....	6.28	87,000,000	5.84	79,382,000	6.32	87,540,000	7.09	97,777,000	6.81	94,448,000
February	....	....	....	....	6.21	85,500,000	6.00	82,189,000	6.45	89,000,000	7.25	99,551,000	7.09	97,777,000
March	....	....	....	....	6.08	83,565,000	5.90	80,797,000	6.39	88,500,000	7.23	99,545,000	7.12	98,177,000
April	....	....	....	....	5.62	75,775,000	5.95	81,300,000	6.60	91,290,000	7.25	99,551,000	7.01	96,954,000
May	....	....	6.02	82,500,000	5.96	81,300,000	6.01	82,189,000	6.52	90,079,000	7.02	96,834,000	6.85	95,000,000
June	....	....	6.02	82,500,000	6.01	82,190,000	6.02	82,200,000	6.20	86,220,000	6.75	93,622,000	7.01	96,954,000
July	5.76	77,960,000	6.00	82,189,000	6.00	82,189,000	6.15	84,917,000	6.36	88,000,000	6.82	94,713,000	7.17	98,695,000
August	6.00	82,189,000	4.96	64,700,000	5.62	76,000,000	6.05	83,000,000	6.19	85,500,000	6.09	83,580,000	7.15	98,395,000
September	....	....	3.50	47,937,000	5.03	65,000,000	6.00	82,189,000	6.38	88,500,000	6.80	93,682,000	7.28	100,000,000
October	....	....	6.13	84,900,000	5.83	79,382,000	6.03	83,000,000	6.19	86,220,000	7.04	97,000,000	7.41	101,080,000
November	....	....	6.00	82,189,000	5.75	77,960,000	5.88	80,000,000	6.17	84,917,000	7.36	100,741,000	7.37	100,941,000
December	....	....	6.37	88,100,000	5.77	78,000,000	6.13	84,917,000	6.17	84,917,000	7.66	102,838,000	7.33	100,341,000

TABLE 2—(Continued).

Average Depth in Aqueduct and Average Delivery in Gallons per day.

Months.	1875.		1876.		1877.		1878.		1879.		1880.		1881.	
	Depth in Aqueduct at Sing Sing.	Delivery of Aqueduct.	Depth in Aqueduct at Sing Sing.	Delivery of Aqueduct.	Depth in Aqueduct at Sing Sing.	Delivery of Aqueduct.	Depth in Aqueduct at Sing Sing.	Delivery of Aqueduct.	Depth in Aqueduct at Sing Sing.	Delivery of Aqueduct.	Depth in Aqueduct at Sing Sing.	Delivery of Aqueduct.	Depth in Aqueduct at Sing Sing.	Delivery of Aqueduct.
	Feet.	Gallons.	Feet.	Gallons.	Feet.	Gallons.	Feet.	Gallons.	Feet.	Gallons.	Feet.	Gallons.	Feet.	Gallons.
January	7.38	100,780,000	7.52	101,866,000	7.09	97,877,000	7.28	99,851,000	7.33	100,341,000	7.34	100,441,000	7.10	97,977,000
February	7.45	101,350,000	7.53	101,926,000	7.35	100,541,000	7.26	99,651,000	7.32	100,241,000	7.33	100,341,000	7.28	99,851,000
March	7.51	101,890,000	7.61	102,518,000	7.35	100,541,000	7.27	99,751,000	7.36	100,641,000	7.35	100,541,000	7.34	100,441,000
April	7.49	101,600,000	7.62	102,578,000	7.43	101,280,000	7.27	99,751,000	7.35	100,541,000	7.35	100,541,000	7.33	100,341,000
May	7.48	101,500,000	7.60	102,458,000	7.45	101,480,000	7.21	99,150,000	7.31	100,141,000	7.32	100,241,000	7.32	100,241,000
June	7.50	101,746,000	7.58	102,338,000	7.32	100,241,000	7.30	100,041,000	7.31	100,141,000	7.25	99,551,000	7.32	100,241,000
July	7.48	101,500,000	7.49	101,686,000	7.12	98,177,000	7.29	99,941,000	7.32	100,241,000	7.07	97,677,000	7.31	100,141,000
August	7.57	102,320,000	6.98	96,784,000	6.81	94,528,000	7.27	99,751,000	7.28	99,851,000	7.17	98,695,000	7.29	99,951,000
September	7.58	102,338,000	5.50	73,617,000	5.01	64,810,000	7.30	100,041,000	7.02	97,004,000	7.19	98,895,000	7.29	99,951,000
October	7.60	102,458,000	5.44	72,743,000	6.26	87,646,000	7.32	100,241,000	7.36	100,641,000	7.12	98,177,000	7.29	99,951,000
November	7.56	102,200,000	6.55	90,679,000	7.30	100,041,000	7.33	100,341,000	7.36	100,641,000	7.23	100,141,000	7.35	100,541,000
December	7.58	102,338,000	6.50	90,079,000	7.26	99,651,000	7.34	100,440,000	7.34	100,441,000	7.09	97,677,000	7.29	99,951,000

TABLE 3.

Rain-fall in Croton Basin.

Months.	1866.			1867.			1868.			1869.			1870.			1871.			1872.			1873.		
	Croton Dam.	Boyd's Corners.	South East.	Croton Dam.	Boyd's Corners.	South East.	Croton Dam.	Boyd's Corners.	South East.	Croton Dam.	Boyd's Corners.	South East.	Croton Dam.	Boyd's Corners.	South East.	Croton Dam.	Boyd's Corners.	South East.	Croton Dam.	Boyd's Corners.	South East.	Croton Dam.	Boyd's Corners.	South East.
January	1.04	3.33	....	1.26	2.11	....	3.23	2.90	....	5.40	3.79	....	9.51	4.51	....	1.18	3.80	....	.76	1.44	....	2.96	5.66	....
February.....	5.58	3.60	....	4.90	3.00	....	1.52	1.38	....	5.75	3.64	...	6.37	6.40	....	.12	3.81	....	1.29	1.22	....	1.40	3.09	....
March	2.15	3.33	....	2.46	1.49	....	3.91	2.55	....	9.51	5.48	....	7.23	3.80	....	5.62	4.27	....	3.57	2.59	....	1.90	3.08	....
April.........	2.69	3.79	....	3.13	3.74	....	5.47	3.87	....	3.38	2.11	....	4.95	5.45	....	4.92	3.01	....	.70	3.04	....	3.17	3.77	....
May..........	5.06	5.62	....	7.26	6.86	....	13.78	8.79	....	6.72	4.52	....	2.71	2.30	....	5.74	3.45	....	3.93	3.69	....	3.02	2.91	....
June	4.41	4.45	....	7.19	5.28	....	7.11	4.53	....	1.19	3.59	....	....	2.06	....	8.62	5.73	....	3.65	4.00	....	.14	.71	....
July..........	4.27	4.01	....	5.22	5.25	....	3.65	2.13	....	2.06	2.26	....	2.75	3.43	....	5.33	5.07	....	5.11	4.34	....	4.44	2.21	....
August.......	5.50	6.56	....	8.79	10.04	....	13.05	6.98	....	1.97	1.92	....	7.71	5.10	....	9.48	5.24	....	7.83	5.99	...	9.91	5.73	....
September....	6.16	4.92	....	3.66	3.62	....	20.47	9.33	....	2.64	3.20	....	2.36	2.85	....	1.47	1.44	....	3.17	3.69	....	5.36	3.73	....
October	4.44	5.09	....	4.74	3.66	....	0.63	0.87	....	8.93	9.46	....	7.62	4.73	....	7.89	6.18	....	1.80	2.15	....	4.85	5.13	....
November....	3.87	3.80	....	3.42	3.10	....	7.14	4.65	....	7.23	2.43	....	3.74	2.51	....	7.71	4.35	....	4.51	4.91	....	2.16	3.72	....
December	3.59	3.27	....	1.98	2.62	....	2.50	2.35	....	5.74	5.96	....	1.20	1.49	....	.42	2.59	....	1.80	3.68	....	2.37	4.13	....
Totals....	48.78	51.77	....	54.03	50.77	....	82.46	50.33	....	60.52	48.36	....	56.15	44.63	....	72.81	48.94	....	43.48	40.74	....	46.08	43.87	....

TABLE 3—(Continued).

RAIN-FALL IN CROTON BASIN.

MONTHS.	1874.			1875.			1876.			1877.		
	Croton Dam.	Boyd's Corners.	South East.	Croton Dam.	Boyd's Corners.	South East.	Croton Dam.	Boyd's Corners.	South East.	Croton Dam.	Boyd's Corners.	South East.
January	5.98	6.96	..	2.01	2.74	..	1.03	1.42	..	3.23	2.68	..
February.....	.17	2.78	..	3.83	3.47	..	6.98	4.91	..	1.21	0.80	..
March	.54	1.57	..	5.87	4.99	..	14.61	6.33	..	8.89	7.66	..
April.........	3.49	6.31	..	3.78	3.04	..	3.78	4.43	..	2.73	2.35	..
May..........	1.59	1.99	..	1.36	1.08	..	3.42	3.99	..	.50	.85	..
June..........	2.26	3.57	..	2.78	3.02	..	4.35	2.52	..	5.58	4.95	..
July..........	5.96	5.98	..	7.34	3.10	..	5.13	3.42	..	6.26	4.65	..
August.......	4.22	2.75	..	12.98	10.33	..	2.51	1.20	..	3.18	2.54	..
September....	4.32	3.56	..	1.76	2.11	..	4.41	5.21	..	1.09	1.49	..
October	1.90	2.40	..	4.27	3.61	..	2.13	1.50	..	10.03	8.38	..
November....	2.68	2.72	..	4.17	4.61	..	3.33	3.40	..	8.06	8.16	..
December	.99	1.78	..	1.76	1.56	..	6.51	2.35	..	1.35	1.52	..
Totals....	36.93	42.37	..	53.52	43.66	..	58.14	40.68	..	52.11	46.03	..

MONTHS.	1878.			1879.			1880.			1881.		
	Croton Dam.	Boyd's Corners.	South East.	Croton Dam.	Boyd's Corners.	South East.	Croton Dam.	Boyd's Corners.	South East.	Croton Dam.	Boyd's Corners.	South East.
January	4.30	4.49	....	4.56	2.52	2.20	3.71	4.00	3.69	5.32	4.19	5.06
February.....	4.61	3.65	....	4.53	2.85	2.47	2.85	2.92	3.13	6.70	5.28	4.65
March	2.69	3.10	....	5.76	4.96	3.85	3.30	4.51	4.21	9.76	6.14	6.16
April.........	4.00	2.85	....	4.17	5.10	4.80	3.28	3.99	3.44	.86	1.67	1.20
May..........	2.69	4.97	1.72	2.19	2.45	2.02	1.10	1.17	1.00	2.74	3.74	3.89
June..........	4.52	4.65	6.13	5.23	5.29	5.36	1.47	1.28	1.43	5.27	5.27	4.62
July..........	3.86	4.28	3.02	5.28	5.95	6.12	6.56	5.65	5.49	1.60	2.45	2.17
August.......	2.63	2.66	4.49	9.39	5.83	6.69	5.25	3.60	4.05	2.97	1.71	3.30
September....	11.26	6.61	8.58	2.88	3.43	3.40	2.64	2.69	2.16	0.41	0.75	0.94
October	6.79	3.78	3.51	0.39	0.95	.57	2.43	3.25	2.56	1.98	3.65	2.75
November....	5.27	4.36	4.43	2.59	2.49	2.54	2.54	2.97	1.85	5.60	4.50	5.53
December	13.28	8.74	7.08	4.80	4.26	3.17	2.38	2.49	2.44	7.56	6.37	8.12
Totals....	65.90	54.14	....	51.77	46.08	43.19	37.51	38.52	35.45	50.77	46.17	48.39

TABLE 4.

Showing Rain-fall and Melted Snow, in Inches, for each Month in the Years 1862 to 1870, inclusive, at Receiving Reservoir, High Bridge, Fordham, Tarrytown, Sing Sing, Croton Dam, and Boyd's Corners.

Months.	1862.							1863.							1864.						
	Receiving Reservoir.	High Bridge.	Fordham.	Tarrytown.	Sing Sing.	Croton Dam.	Boyd's Corners.	Receiving Reservoir.	High Bridge.	Fordham.	Tarrytown.	Sing Sing.	Croton Dam.	Boyd's Corners.	Receiving Reservoir.	High Bridge.	Fordham.	Tarrytown.	Sing Sing.	Croton Dam.	Boyd's Corners.
January	3.77	....	4.45	4.88	....	4.75	....	3.23	....	4.41	....	....	5.25	....	1.83	....	2.06	1.59	3.01	1.84	....
February	2.33	....	3.25	2.91	....	2.88	....	3.61	....	5.74	....	....	0.10	....	0.95	....	1.00	1.26	1.95	1.49	....
March	4.46	....	4.60	3.25	....	2.17	....	4.46	....	5.77	....	....	3.16	....	2.03	....	2.65	2.35	4.50	5.49	....
April	1.59	....	3.28	1.82	....	0.55	....	4.72	....	3.91	....	....	4.31	....	2.24	....	3.89	3.16	7.49	3.04	....
May	2.85	....	3.36	2.28	....	....	....	4.58	....	5.32	....	....	3.99	....	4.52	....	5.17	4.54	10.59	4.95	....
June	5.75	....	3.19	5.65	....	....	....	1.68	....	3.29	....	....	0.52	....	4.59	....	3.08	2.14	5.07	1.76	....
July	4.32	....	5.83	6.13	....	5.42	....	6.18	....	6.25	....	....	10.27	....	1.85	....	2.20	2.61	4.61	2.42	....
August	2.45	....	2.59	1.76	....	2.18	....	4.91	....	2.40	....	....	4.78	....	2.12	....	5.98	7.88	11.81	7.45	....
September	3.75	....	1.91	1.73	2.33	2.17	....	1.03	....	0.82	....	....	1.39	....	5.09	....	5.19	4.49	6.86	3.66	....
October	4.23	....	5.24	3.42	3.04	3.37	....	3.12	....	3.48	....	....	4.99	....	2.47	....	2.70	2.69	5.72	2.97	....
November	4.75	....	4.55	4.69	4.94	5.98	....	1.76	....	3.55	....	....	4.37	....	3.88	....	4.82	4.00	8.95	3.48	....
December	1.28	....	1.57	0.57	....	0.98	....	3.58	....	4.89	5.29	6.65	4.10	....	2.83	....	3.05	3.09	2.90	2.73	....
Total	41.53	....	43.82	39.09	....	30.45	....	42.86	....	49.83	....	....	47.23	....	34.70	....	41.79	39.80	73.46	41.28	....
Mean	3.46	....	3.65	3.26	....	2.54	....	3.57	....	4.15	....	....	3.94	....	2.89	....	3.48	3.32	6.12	3.44	....

TABLE 4—(Continued).

Showing Rain-fall and Melted Snow, in Inches, for each Month in the Years 1862 to 1870, inclusive, at Receiving Reservoir, High Bridge, Fordham, Tarrytown, Sing Sing, Croton Dam, and Boyd's Corners.

Months.	1865.							1866.							1867.						
	Receiving Reservoir.	High Bridge.	Fordham.	Tarrytown.	Sing Sing.	Croton Dam.	Boyd's Corners.	Receiving Reservoir.	High Bridge.	Fordham.	Tarrytown.	Sing Sing.	Croton Dam.	Boyd's Corners.	Receiving Reservoir.	High Bridge.	Fordham.	Tarrytown.	Sing Sing.	Croton Dam.	Boyd's Corners.
January	2.66	....	3.60	3.19	4.47	3.43	....	1.01	....	1.48	1.33	0.85	1.04	3.33	3.34	0.61	1.32	0.89	0.20	1.26	2.11
February	3.79	....	4.54	3.24	3.81	2.86	....	5.38	....	5.78	4.48	7.22	5.58	3.60	5.15	4.79	5.87	4.12	8.34	4.92	3.00
March	4.85	....	5.83	4.03	8.03	5.03	....	2.44	....	2.47	2.10	2.60	2.15	3.33	5.24	2.53	3.63	2.20	2.40	2.46	1.49
April	3.77	....	3.81	2.94	4.25	2.95	....	2.66	....	3.25	2.68	2.48	2.69	3.79	2.50	2.15	2.96	2.91	6.68	3.13	3.74
May	4.91	....	5.51	6.37	13.88	7.38	....	4.33	....	4.09	4.57	9.12	5.06	5.62	5.78	3.55	6.34	6.15	9.85	7.26	6.86
June	3.72	....	4.88	6.60	6.05	3.41	....	2.68	....	3.21	3.39	7.78	4.41	4.45	9.45	9.21	9.24	6.09	20.15	7.19	5.28
July	5.73	....	5.80	8.64	16.18	3.05	....	4.13	....	4.36	3.63	7.87	4.27	4.01	4.50	4.90	4.34	4.48	5.14	5.22	5.25
August	3.16	....	2.55	3.30	5.31	8.12	....	5.48	....	6.03	6.72	8.42	5.50	6.56	8.54	9.14	11.04	8.81	15.18	8.79	10.04
September	1.77	....	1.85	2.71	3.34	2.23	....	3.69	....	4.59	6.23	9.22	6.18	4.92	0.77	0.65	0.66	0.24	1.59	3.66	3.62
October	3.93	....	4.85	3.63	8.35	4.56	....	5.41	....	5.16	5.71	5.60	4.44	5.09	3.73	4.77	5.87	4.84	8.64	4.74	3.95
November	2.69	....	4.14	3.48	6.30	3.15	....	3.16	....	2.87	3.08	6.75	3.87	3.80	1.98	2.45	2.59	2.74	6.53	3.42	3.10
December	4.16	....	4.95	3.76	5.20	3.87	....	3.04	....	4.04	3.38	7.79	3.59	3.27	2.34	2.27	2.43	2.26	3.32	1.98	1.62
Total	45.14	....	52.31	51.29	84.07	50.04	....	43.41	....	47.31	47.30	75.70	48.78	51.77	53.32	47.08	56.29	45.73	88.02	54.03	50.07
Mean	3.76	....	4.36	4.32	7.06	4.17	...	3.62	....	3.94	3.93	6.31	4.07	4.31	4.44	3.92	4.69	3.81	7.35	4.50	4.17

TABLE 4—(Continued).

Showing Rain-fall and Melted Snow, in Inches, for each Month in the Years 1862 to 1870, inclusive, at Receiving Reservoir, High Bridge, Fordham, Tarrytown, Sing Sing, Croton Dam, and Boyd's Corners.

Months.	1868.							1869.							1870.						
	Receiving Reservoir.	High Bridge.	Fordham.	Tarrytown.	Sing Sing.	Croton Dam.	Boyd's Corners.	Receiving Reservoir.	High Bridge.	Fordham.	Tarrytown.	Sing Sing.	Croton Dam.	Boyd's Corners.	Receiving Reservoir.	High Bridge.	Fordham.	Tarrytown.	Sing Sing.	Croton Dam.	Boyd's Corners.
January	4.53	5.57	4.03	5.20	5.72	3.23	2.90	2.99	3.47	3.68	4.74	3.95	5.40	3.79	4.83	5.85	6.06	4.70	14.18	9.51	4.51
February	2.32	0.36	2.91	1.10	2.65	1.52	1.38	5.84	5.75	7.50	4.83	3.80	5.75	3.64	5.15	2.90	3.75	5.11	6.24	6.37	6.40
March	0.35	0.75	4.34	2.09	1.67	3.91	2.55	4.38	4.01	6.33	5.06	10.64	9.51	5.48	4.34	5.18	5.22	2.64	8.90	7.23	3.80
April	6.09	5.29	6.92	4.06	8.24	5.47	3.87	1.87	1.39	1.85	1.96	2.72	3.38	2.11	4.40	4.56	4.77	4.80	6.40	4.95	5.45
May	6.14	10.41	3.30	7.99	12.26	13.78	8.79	4.39	4.14	4.14	4.38	7.64	6.72	4.52	2.06	2.11	2.05	3.19	6.00	2.71	2.30
June	4.80	4.95	6.60	5.06	8.86	7.11	4.53	4.38	6.37	6.37	2.74	4.62	1.19	3.59	2.66	2.50	2.07	2.77	7.05	....	2.06
July	5.58	7.22	6.39	5.94	4.95	3.65	2.13	3.83	3.82	3.28	2.66	3.82	2.06	2.26	3.53	....	3.33	2.98	4.16	2.75	3.43
August	8.65	4.86	4.51	5.86	14.70	13.05	6.98	2.49	5.31	3.13	3.02	4.55	1.97	1.92	3.24	4.24	4.46	6.83	7.69	7.71	5.10
September	9.30	9.09	9.76	10.19	21.97	20.47	9.33	2.46	3.57	3.00	2.70	5.61	2.64	3.20	2.02	2.43	3.04	1.16	2.76	2.36	2.85
October	1.32	1.37	2.38	0.72	0.16	0.63	0.87	7.03	7.65	8.45	7.84	16.98	8.93	9.46	4.90	4.83	5.19	6.18	6.95	7.62	4.73
November	4.28	4.90	5.32	4.30	7.60	7.14	4.65	3.28	3.55	3.53	2.70	10.03	7.23	2.43	2.71	2.96	2.84	2.55	4.04	3.74	2.51
December	2.77	2.56	3.26	2.68	4.64	2.50	2.35	5.47	5.47	5.10	7.77	8.62	5.74	5.96	2.49	2.31	2.11	1.96	1.33	1.20	1.49
Total	56.13	57.33	59.72	55.19	93.42	82.46	50.33	48.41	54.50	56.36	50.40	82.98	60.52	48.36	42.33	39.87	44.89	44.87	75.70	56.15	44.63
Mean	4.68	4.78	4.98	4.59	7.79	6.88	4.19	4.04	4.54	4.69	4.20	6.92	5.04	4.03	3.53	3.32	3.74	3.74	6.31	4.68	3.72

TABLE 5.

Comparison of Rain-fall at Different Places.

	1866.	1867.	1868.	1869.	1870.	1871.	1872.	1873.	1874.	1875.	1876.	1877.	1878.	1879.	1880.	1881.
Croton Dam......	48.78	54.03	82.46	52	56.15	72.81	43.48	46.08	36.93	53.52	58.14	52.11	65.90	51.77	37.51	50.77
Boyd's Corners....	51.77	50.77	50.33	48.36	44.63	48.94	40.74	43.87	42.37	43.66	40.68	46.03	54.14	46.08	38.52	46.17
Southeast	.....	.....	.....	.....	.....	.....	.....	.....	.....	.....	....	....	....	43.19	35.45	48.39
Sing Sing.........	75.70	88.02	93.42	82.98	76.54	91.35	55.60	66.94	71.87	75.90	66.24	....	....	....	....	.....
Tarrytown........	47.30	45.73	55.19	50.40	47.50	60.39	42.75	50.44	49.38	59.58	47.74	....	....	....	....	.....
Kingsbridge	47.31	56.29	59.72	56.36	45.09	57.90	48.43	52.36	51.12	52.44	43.32	....	....	....	....	....
West Point.......	47.51	57.83	52.11	47.64	42.33	52.41	56.38	44.83	47.60	54.09	48.11	47.76	48.78	42.59	33.53	46.30
Central Park Observatory.....	52.23	54.66	64.03	45.47	39.25	51.26	42.49	47.99	45.83	40.90	41.77	40.18	48.66	39.03	36.64	36.26
Central Park Receiving Res...	43.40	53.32	56.13	48.41	42.45	53.07	47.02	49.71	52.86	45.31	38.91	42.97	49.86	38.66	36.14	36.86

TABLE 6.

Showing Rain-fall and Melted Snow at North Salem Croton Basin, N. Y.; Latitude, 41° 20′; Longitude, 73° 38′; Elevation, 361 feet.

Year.	January.	February.	March.	April.	May.	June.	July.	August.	September.	October.	November.	December.	Total Fall of Rain and Melted Snow.	Average per Month.	Driest Month in the Year.	Wettest Month in the Year.
	Inches.	Inches.	Inches.	Inches.	Inches.	Inches.	Inches.	Inches.	Inches.	Inches.	Inches.	Inches.	Inches.	Inches.		
1830	2.18	1.82	5.05	1.76	3.29	5.97	5.50	0.41	2.25	4.81	3.41	6.92	43.37	3.61	August	December.
1831	2.09	2.54	2.38	5.79	3.41	3.31	4.39	3.22	4.50	6.51	3.02	0.60	41.76	3.48	December	October.
1832	3.18	1.61	3.40	2.97	3.58	1.25	3.65	7.99	2.25	3.78	3.60	3.67	40.93	3.41	June	August.
1833	3.17	1.13	3.34	1.57	5.11	3.89	3.01	2.69	3.06	9.90	1.97	4.21	43.05	3.58	February	October.
1834	1.52	0.82	1.28	4.38	4.44	7.02	4.45	0.31	4.75	2.15	0.83	1.57	33.50	2.60	August	June.
1835	6.12	0.82	1.77	6.25	1.46	1.96	5.52	2.07	1.44	3.42	1.88	2.78	35.49	2.96	February	April.
1838	2.45	0.96	1 52	2.04	3.48	3.48	1.79	1.73	5.14	3.42	3.91	0.95	30.87	2.57	December	September.
1840	1.46	1.92	2.45	4.18	3.63	3.52	2.95	3.19	2.70	5.82	2.81	3.91	38.54	3.21	January	October.
1841	6.20	1.70	2.51	4.38	2.54	2.93	1.87	1.78	2.06	4.08	4.17	5.56	39.78	3.31	February	January.
1842	1.55	4.78	1.50	4.95	4.99	2.77	5.56	6.05	3.80	4.57	2.53	2.67	45.72	3.81	March	August.
1843	2.51	3.27	5.53	4.03	2.06	2.58	3.99	8.74	5.00	5.80	3.90	1.50	48.91	4.08	May	August.
1844	2.77	0.88	4.44	1.73	5.49	2.67	6.63	1.59	1.96	4.33	1.23	3.57	37.49	3.12	February	July.
1845	4.94	2.87	2.37	1.62	2.60	2.05	2.36	3.40	3.84	4.17	5.48	3.80	39.50	3.30	April	November.
1846	4.07	2.65	3.71	1.95	6.90	3.43	7.20	5.11	0.35	2.59	4.78	2.93	45.67	3.80	September	July.
1847	3.61	5.41	3.76	1.28	2.05	3.00	5.00	3.25	5.33	3.61	3.02	4.88	44.80	3.73	April	February.
1848	1.46	1.60	2.05	1.23	7.02	4.41	4.27	1.27	2.06	2.56	2.81	3.88	34.62	2.88	April	May.
1849	1.55	2.09	5.19	1.35	5.85	1.09	1.32	7.24	1.43	7.88	4.42	3.24	42.65	3.55	June	October.
1850	4.46	4.67	3.68	2.73	7.60	5.41	6.81	4.97	6.63	1.64	3.03	3.39	55.02	4.58	October	May.
Mean	3.07	2.27	3.11	3.01	4.19	3.46	4.23	3.61	3.08	4.50	2.29	3.30	42.41	....	February	October.

August, 1834, Driest Month of this Period .... 0.31 inches.
October, 1833, Wettest Month of this Period .... 9.90 "
Average Annual Rain-fall .... 42.41 "
Average Driest Month, February, Mean .... 2.27 "
Next Driest M,tonh November, Mean .... 2.29 "

Average Wettest Month, October .... 4.50 inches.
Next Wettest Month, July .... 4.23 "

The above is taken from page 330 of "N. Y. Meteorology," by F. B. Hough, from Reports of Regents of University.

FROM REPORT OF DR. DANIEL DRAPER, 1876.

THE DROUGHT OF 1876.

The most important meteorological phenomenon for the past year was the drought that caused great scarcity of Croton water in this city. It began with an unusually small fall of rain, the total amount for January being .94 inch, while the average for forty-one years is 3.30 inches. There are only two other years on record in which the rain-fall for that month was less ; they are 1839, when it was .69 inch, and 1849, when it was .61 inch. The following two months were above their averages, February having 4.81 inches, its average for forty-one years being 3.40 inches, while in March it was 8.79 inches, the average being 3.76. After this all the other months were below their averages, except September, which was 1.60 above, as is shown in Table 7.

TABLE 7.

TABLE *showing Monthly and Annual Fall of Water for* 46 *years, in the Vicinity of New York City* (*at Fort Columbus, Deaf and Dumb Asylum, and New York Observatory, Central Park*).

INCHES.

	YEAR.	JAN.	FEB.	MAR.	APRIL	MAY.	JUNE.	JULY.	AUG.	SEPT.	OCT.	NOV.	DEC.	ANNUAL AMOUNT.
Army Records.	1836......	1.09	2.01	1.31	2.66	0.63	6.46	1.44	2.37	3.40	2.00	1.90	2.30	27.57
	1837......	2.70	3.70	8.20	7.50	9.50	8.50	5.90	6.30	2.10	2.11	2.90	6.10	65.51
	1838......	3.93	3.70	4.10	2.50	3.99	3.12	1.83	4.79	4.96	3.64	3.10	2.24	41.90
	1839......	0.69	2.05	2.46	3.35	8.37	4.94	1.35	4.92	3.59	1.45	2.19	7.61	42.97
	1840......	1.84	1.84	2.92	2.03	2.39	2.40	1.80	4.25	1.84	4.59	2.90	1.00	29.80
	1841......	5.30	0.80	2.35	3.93	3.95	4.65	4.90	2.50	2.90	4.40	3.70	2.70	42.08
	1842......	1.07	2.85	1.25	3.60	3.69	3.30	3.80	2.81	2.10	4.30	1.80	3.50	33.98
	1843......	1.00	2.31	2.13	2.14	1.00	0.76	1.64	15.26	3.06	5.91	2.82	3.34	41.37
	1844......	2.66	1.03	4.50	0.55	3.41	2.37	6.00	2.73	4.50	4.08	1.73	2.82	36.38
	1845......	4.87	3.22	3.33	1.22	1.75	3.70	1.75	3.21	2.62	2.50	3.40	2.51	34.08
	1846......	3.92	3.01	3.82	4.01	9.70	1.39	6.01	3.88	0.48	1.34	8.36	2.99	48.91
	1847......	4.62	5.74	8.48	1.53	2.18	6.78	1.62	6.93	12.20	2.13	6.29	6.35	64.85
	1848......	1.75	1.68	2.23	1.16	7.28	4.56	2.64	1.41	1.87	6.61	1.59	4.02	36.80
	1849......	0.61	2.26	4.87	0.62	3.47	0.78	1.43	4.63	1.55	5.63	1.88	4.01	31.74
	1850......	5.57	2.64	4.64	2.72	9.20	3.07	3.92	7.21	4.71	3.16	2.33	5.36	54.53
	1851......	1.46	4.50	1.70	6.94	4.73	0.90	4.72	3.47	1.26	2.95	4.53	3.72	40.88
	1852......	2.92	3.08	4.43	4.74	2.24	2.11	3.25	6.20	2.29	2.06	6.07	4.45	43.84
	1853......	4.14	4.98	2.03	3.32	5.80	4.80	4.40	5.50	5.49	3.90	6.80	1.04	52.20
	1854......	2.60	4.00	0.70	8.80	7.70	2.20	1.90	1.03	1.90	1.80	3.95	8.60	45.18
Deaf and Dumb.	1855......	4.77	5.12	2.83	2.86	4.90	5.83	5.06	2.90	1.51	7.37	3.00	6.86	53.01
	1856......	3.98	0.66	2.08	2.72	4.78	3.58	2.79	6.73	5.05	1.18	2.50	4.45	40.50
	1857......	4.99	1.69	2.32	9.05	6.72	5.43	6.13	3.90	4.26	1.67	1.30	6.42	53.88
	1858......	3.80	3.30	1.47	4.83	6.00	6.42	4.32	3.15	3.50	4.19	5.99	4.90	51.87
	1859......	5.78	5.59	8.21	5.10	1.57	4.60	4.76	4.12	6.45	1.75	3.37	4.42	55.72
	1860......	2.52	3.28	1.60	3.21	4.54	1.43	3.33	3.85	6.24	3.55	7.57	4.05	45.17
	1861......	4.81	2.45	5.78	5.62	6.03	4.24	2.89	5.52	4.03	3.46	8.09	1.73	54.65
	1862......	5.60	4.17	4.54	2.14	3.84	9.03	5.85	2.15	2.25	6.86	5.63	1.91	53.97
	1863......	5.45	7.04	5.77	5.69	4.58	1.43	8.60	4.59	1.05	4.09	3.88	4.86	57.03
	1864......	2.92	2.04	2.15	3.28	5.23	4.41	3.20	5.19	5.45	2.68	5.16	5.90	47.61
	1865......	3.40	4.06	8.32	4.14	5.56	10.42	5.21	2.23	4.21	4.94	4.19	6.30	62.98
	1866......	2.56	10.09	2.28	4.09	4.46	4.38	1.67	4.81	4.85	5.28	3.84	3.92	52.23
	1867......	2.54	5.53	4.09	2.47	5.70	10.18	5.76	7.68	0.78	5.12	2.25	2.56	54.66
	1868......	4.00	2.31	3.69	6.42	7.19	4.66	6.44	8.31	9.60	2.01	5.13	4.27	64.03
Central Park.	1869......	2.53	6.87	4.61	1.39	4.15	4.40	3.15	1.76	2.81	6.48	2.30	5.02	45.47
	1870......	4.41	2.83	3.33	5.11	1.83	2.82	3.76	3.07	2.52	4.97	2.42	2.18	39.25
	1871......	2.07	2.72	5.54	3.03	4.04	7.05	5.57	5.60	2.34	7.50	3.56	2.24	51.26
	1872......	1.88	1.29	3.74	2.29	2.68	2.93	7.83	6.29	2.95	3.35	4.08	3.18	42.49
	1873......	5.34	3.80	2.09	4.16	3.69	1.28	4.61	9.56	3.14	2.73	4.63	2.96	47.99
	1874......	5.33	2.04	2.12	8.77	2.24	2.78	5.06	2.43	8.24	1.70	2.30	2.82	45.83
	1875......	3.17	2.62	3.48	3.08	1.33	2.72	4.89	8.97	1.89	2.85	3.78	2.12	40.90
	1876......	0.94	4.81	8.79	3.06	3.03	2.66	3.65	2.28	5.28	1.42	3.31	2.54	41.77
	1877......	2.62	1.24	5.56	2.73	0.95	2.80	5.73	2.77	1.33	8.14	5.63	0.68	40.18
	1878......	4.46	3.75	3.27	1.97	3.19	3.08	4.62	7.97	4.05	2.43	4.73	5.14	48.66
	1879......	2.63	2.02	3.41	4.33	2.02	3.15	3.58	7.95	2.37	.43	2.20	4.94	39.03
	1880......	2.02	2.12	4.66	2.90	.62	1.14	8.53	5.26	1.85	2.81	2.46	2.27	36.64
	1881......	4.80	4.93	5.81	0.95	3.20	5.35	1.25	.86	.97	1.60	2.36	4.18	36.26

This drought has led me to examine the following question:

Has there been in late years any change in the rain-fall of New York City or its vicinity to affect seriously its water supply?

In a former report I discussed a question nearly related to this, viz.: "Does the clearing of land increase or diminish the fall of rain." We found that the wide-spread impression that the clearing of land diminishes the volume of rain is not based on fact. We shall have to study the present question in a similar manner, relying on the observations then used, and others that have since been collected.

As the water supply of New York comes from the Croton river, we shall have to examine the table of the rain-fall on the shed of that river, but as the observations for it extend back only a few years, it becomes necessary to compare them with those of New York City.

The annual observations at Boyd's Corners, which is within the Croton water-shed, are from 1870 to 1877, and those of this Observatory are for the same period. By the table it appears that the rain-fall of these stations varies from year to year, but in the means for the series there is a variation of only 1.8 inch. This might be expected from topographical and other considerations.

Years.	1871.	1872.	1873.	1874.	1875.	1876.	Mean.
Boyd's Corners......	48.94	40.74	43.87	42.37	43.66	40.68	43.37
Central Park	51.26	42.49	47.99	45.83	40.90	41.77	45.17

The fall at Boyd's Corners resembles that of the city. We may therefore use our city observations for the missing ones there.

The fall in New York City bears, in like manner, a general resemblance to that of other adjacent cities, as Washington, Philadelphia, Providence; and since there exist very old observations made in those places, they may be used in investigating the rain-falls here. Of course it will be understood that I am not here speaking of the absolute rain-falls in those places, but the variations they exhibit, and using those variations as a guide to the determination in New York.

TABLE 8.

Monthly and Annual Fall of Rain, from January, 1865, to December, 1881, at Receiving Reservoir, Central Park.

Months.	1865.		1866.		1867.		1868.		1869.		1870.		1871.		1872.		1873.	
	Rain or Melted Snow. Inches.	Depth of Snow. Inches.	Rain or Melted Snow. Inches.	Depth of Snow. Inches.	Rain or Melted Snow. Inches.	Depth of Snow. Inches.	Rain cr Melted Snow. Inches.	Depth of Snow. Inches.	Rain or Melted Snow. Inches.	Depth of Snow. Inches.	Rain or Melted Snow. Inches.	Depth of Snow. Inches.	Rain or Melted Snow. Inches.	Depth of Snow. Inches.	Rain or Melted Snow. Inches.	Depth of Snow. Inches.	Rain or Melted Snow. Inches.	Depth of Snow. Inches.
January	2.71	6½	1.01	8¾	3.34	27¼	4.53	25¾	2.99	7½	4.83	3	4.10	21	1.90	2¾	5.91	12
February	3.79	8¾	5.28	7¼	5.15	13	2.32	15¼	6.04	11½	5.15	9½	4.03	18¼	1.69	4	3.95	16
March	4.85	¼	3.34	2	5.24	12¼	3.35	26	4.98	3¾	4.34	11¼	5.74	....	4.08	4	2.35	1
April	4.77	....	2.66	....	2.25	....	6.09	7¾	1.88	....	4.40	....	3.15	2	2.51	¾	3.87	....
May	6.17	....	4.30	....	5.78	....	6.14	....	4.34	....	2.06	....	4.06	....	3.12	....	3.96	....
June	3.77	....	2.68	....	9.45	....	4.80	....	4.33	....	2.78	....	8.05	....	2.80	....	1.18	....
July	5.63	....	4.13	....	4.50	....	5.58	....	3.83	....	3.53	....	6.04	....	8.70	....	6.00	....
August	3.16	....	5.48	....	8.54	....	8.65	....	2.49	....	3.24	....	6.30	....	6.61	....	7.84	....
September	2.46	....	3.69	....	0.77	....	9.30	....	2.46	....	2.02	....	2.41	....	3.61	....	4.04	....
October	4.93	....	4.77	....	3.73	....	1.32	....	7.03	....	4.90	....	8.05	....	2.94	....	3.40	....
November	2.69	....	3.16	....	1.98	....	4.28	....	3.28	....	2.71	....	4.60	½	4.51	4¼	4.77	1½
December	4.36	10	2.71	3¼	2.34	12	2.77	8½	5.47	6¾	2.49	5	2.10	7	4.57	24¾	2.38	7
	49.29	25½	43.21	21¼	53.07	64½	59.13	83¼	49.12	29½	42.45	28¾	58.63	48¾	47.04	40½	49.65	37½

TABLE 8—(Continued).

Monthly ana Annual Fall of Rain, from January, 1865, to December, 1881, at Receiving Reservoir, Central Park.

MONTHS.	1874.		1875.		1876.		1877.		1878.		1879.		1880.		1881.	
	Rain or Melted Snow. Inches.	Depth of Snow. Inches.	Rain or Melted Snow. Inches.	Depth of Snow. Inches.	Rain or Melted Snow. Inches.	Depth of Snow. Inches.	Rain or Melted Snow. Inches.	Depth of Snow. Inches.	Rain or Melted Snow. Inches.	Depth of Snow. Inches.	Rain or Melted Snow. Inches.	Depth of Snow. Inches.	Rain or Melted Snow. Inches.	Depth of Snow. Inches.	Rain or Melted Snow. Inches.	Depth of Snow. Inches.
January	5.81	6¼	2.84	12¾	1.09	....	3.77	18	3.54	¼	3.06	14½	2.16	3½	4.75	12
February............	3.37	16½	3.44	5¾	4.48	10	1.79	....	4.04	6	2.55	15	3.19	1	4.14	8
March	4.09	2	3.15	17½	8.01	2½	6.43	7¾	3.17	....	3.85	...	4.84	10	4.97	3
April	9.47	....	3.37	12½	2.87	....	2.63	....	1.88	....	6.41	....	2.74	....	1.02	...
May	2.62	....	1.85	....	3.34	....	1.04	....	2.75	....	2.09	....	0.62	....	2.86	....
June............	4.69	....	3.21	....	3.93	...	2.73	....	4.18	....	3.10	....	1.01	....	5.75	....
July	6.07	....	4.86	....	2.49	....	5.96	....	6.18	....	2.22	....	7.26	....	1.53	....
August............	2.63	....	11.10	....	2.40	....	2.88	....	8.00	....	6.50	....	4.69	....	1.25	...
September............	7.13	....	1.94	....	3.98	....	1.22	....	3.52	....	2.73	....	1.34	....	1.30	....
October	1.96	....	3.18	....	1.56	....	8.02	....	2.66	....	0.35	....	3.04	....	1.83	....
November............	2.13	....	4.12	....	3.18	¾	5.75	....	4.51	....	2.03	2	2.54	2¾	2.85	....
December	2.89	11½	2.25	3½	1.58	11½	0.75	....	5.43	2	3.77	6	2.71	12	4.61	2
	52.86	36¼	45.31	52	38.91	24¾	42.97	25¾	49.86	8¼	38.66	37½	36.14	29¼	36.86	25

ANNUAL AMOUNT.	
Year.	
1865.......	49.29
1866.......	43.21
1867.......	53.07
1868.......	59.13
1869.......	49.12
1870.......	42.45
1871.......	58.63
1872.......	47.04
1873	49.65
1874.......	52.86
1875.......	45.31
1876.......	38.91
1877.......	42.97
1878.......	49.86
1879.......	38.66
1880.......	36.14
1881.......	36.86

TABLE 9.

Rain-fall at West Point, New York, from 1843 to 1881.

	1843.	1844.	1845.	1846.	1847.	1848.	1849.	1850.	1851.	1852.	1853.	1854.	1855.	1856.	1857.	1858.	1859.	1860.	1861.
January............	2.85	5.25	5.15	3.42	4.01	1.87	1.03	6.06	.82	1.62	3.27	3.62	3.63	1.81	2.25	3.83	4.00	.65	4.25
February...........	3.02	3.10	2.88	2.78	6.22	3.98	2.07	3.33	5.09	3.80	4.45	5.04	4.23	.63	1.79	.65	2.30	4.72	1.80
March..............	5.05	4.20	3.40	3.90	3.49	2.71	4.55	4.84	2.56	2.68	3.25	2.81	.83	1.68	1.88	.92	5.85	.95	3.67
April...............	3.40	.50	1.80	3.04	.79	1.50	.96	4.30	7.24	4.66	5.84	10.53	2.52	3.76	5.32	4.48	4.00	4.25	3.75
May................	2.28	5.10	4.10	2.93	2.70	7.15	6.10	8.26	4.34	1.65	8.04	5.08	4.16	6.59	5.70	6.17	2.89	4.90	3.00
June................	1.95	3.45	1.82	.17	2.27	7.37	1.06	3.97	1.53	2.30	3.79	1.62	4.50	4.81	6.38	4.30	5.49	6.20	2.60
July................	3.00	7.96	2.38	2.46	2.52	4.42	3.15	5.33	4.44	4.67	9.48	3.73	6.26	2.42	2.04	3.22	1.65	5.66	4.70
August.............	11.33	5.28	7.72	10.02	2.20	.49	5.74	5.13	2.58	6.99	7.25	.46	3.10	11.56	3.97	3.52	6.70	3.80	3.50
September	3.62	3.50	2.60	2.80	3.58	3.67	.42	8.14	1.22	2.39	3.89	4.00	.97	4.52	4.46	2.05	5.20	3.70	4.05
October............	6.95	4.92	2.93	2.60	1.97	4.33	7.63	2.14	4.02	2.99	2.85	1.98	10.25	1.35	5.40	3.65	1.55	5.30	2.80
November..........	4.60	1.65	5.36	3.65	1.80	6.76	2.31	2.17	4.31	2.60	5.60	5.65	3.69	2.50	2.75	6.30	2.70	5.35	3.90
December	2.70	4.12	3.24	4.40	3.50	5.04	4.11	5.65	2.45	0.17	2.26	2.64	5.14	5.76	5.55	3.90	1.40	2.73	1.21
Yearly Rain-fall..	50.75	49.03	43.38	42.17	35.05	49.69	39.13	59.32	40.60	36.52	59.97	47.16	49.28	47.39	47.49	42.99	43.73	48.21	39.23

TABLE 9—(Continued).

Rain-fall at West Point, New York, from 1843 to 1881.

	1862.	1863.	1864.	1865.	1866.	1867.	1868.	1869.	1870.	1871.	1872.	1873.	1874.	1875.	1876.	1877.	1878.	1879.	1880.	1881.
January	5.47	5.55	1.10	3.20	1.00	1.15	1.50	2.40	4.90	1.48	1.70	6.82	7.03	3.02	1.45	3.37	4.16	2.21	3.30	5.45
February	2.32	2.84	1.75	1.25	4.50	4.40	1.60	3.50	6.15	2.87	1.00	4.80	2.06	4.24	6.48	1.42	3.15	2.10	3.25	4.30
March	2.90	2.65	3.00	5.25	3.65	1.25	3.86	4.25	4.65	5.24	2.40	2.36	2.08	4.22	9.31	7.40	3.38	4.29	2.25	5.15
April	2.60	2.65	6.00	4.55	3.20	3.40	4.80	3.07	5.15	3.43	3.20	3.82	6.49	3.33	4.38	4.00	3.48	6.04	3.25	.20
May	2.70	5.35	4.65	2.25	4.20	10.50	11.66	4.75	3.82	3.85	5.41	3.31	2.15	1.13	3.37	1.02	5.37	2.20	1.13	4.40
June	9.60	1.90	2.50	4.88	8.51	6.00	3.45	5.33	3.15	7.27	6.16	.76	2.17	3.48	3.49	5.15	3.20	6.25	1.35	5.40
July	4.02	5.90	2.80	4.35	2.90	6.15	1.15	2.43	2.53	8.50	2.10	2.46	8.49	4.31	6.40	4.02	3.37	2.25	5.35	2.25
August	3.00	3.93	5.35	1.65	5.50	11.75	7.20	1.90	2.95	6.60	10.43	4.41	3.10	8.32	.05	2.46	2.35	5.30	4.05	3.00
September	4.30	3.65	2.15	3.05	7.20	6.90	11.22	3.35	2.40	1.03	5.27	3.34	5.36	1.98	4.47	2.16	4.11	3.20	1.45	1.15
October	4.70	4.75	1.35	3.60	2.10	2.00	.90	7.80	3.52	4.96	4.10	5.75	2.33	4.18	2.00	9.34	4.46	.35	2.45	5.30
November	4.56	4.90	3.80	2.70	3.45	3.50	3.85	3.82	1.11	4.40	9.23	2.75	3.33	14.06	3.36	6.06	4.28	3.40	3.30	3.50
December	2.80	4.85	2.60	3.75	1.30	.83	.92	4.99	2.00	2.78	5.38	4.25	3.01	1.82	3.35	1.36	7.47	5.00	2.40	6.20
Yearly Rain-fall	48.97	48.92	37.05	40.48	47.51	57.83	52.11	47.64	42.33	52.41	56.38	44.83	47.60	54.09	48.11	47.76	48.78	42.59	33.53	46.30

TABLE 10.

STORAGE DRAWN IN 1880 AND 1881, IN MILLION GALLONS.

	January.	February.	March.	April.	May.	June.	July.		August.		September.		October.		November	December.
	1881.	1881.				1880.	1880.	1881.	1880.	1881.	1880.	1881.	1880.	1881.	1880.	1880.
1......	60	10	..	..	..	..	75	..	20	50	..	90	85	90	..	..
2......	50	10	..	..	..	..	75	..	30	50	20	90	85	90	..	..
3......	50	10	..	..	..	..	75	..	50	50	60	90	80	90	..	..
4......	50	30	..	..	..	..	75	..	60	50	80	90	80	70	..	..
5......	50	30	..	..	..	..	45	..	75	50	80	90	80	60	..	..
6......	30	30	..	..	..	..	15	..	75	60	80	90	80	70	..	..
7......	30	35	..	..	..	..	25	..	75	30	85	90	80	70	..	..
8......	30	30	..	...	..	..	35	..	75	30	85	90	80	70	..	..
9......	30	30	..	..	..	..	65	..	75	30	85	90	80	70	..	..
10......	30	10	..	..	..	..	70	..	75	60	80	90	80	70	..	..
11......	30	..	..	..	..	..	85	..	75	60	20	90	75	70	..	..
12......	30	..	..	..	..	10	85	..	75	70	25	90	75	90	..	..
13......	..	..	..	..	..	10	65	..	60	80	25	90	75	90	..	..
14......	..	..	..	..	..	30	35	..	60	80	25	90	75	90	..	..
15.....	..	..	..	..	..	30	65	..	60	90	25	90	75	90	..	..
16......		..	..	..	..	40	65	..	45	90	25	90	75	90	..	..
17......	..	..	..	..	..	45	45	..	40	90	15	90	70	90	..	..
18......	..	..	..	..	..	45	15	..	70	90	35	90	70	90	..	..
19......	..	..	..	..	..	45	15	..	75	90	35	90	70	90	..	..
20......	..	..	..	..	..	45	25	30	85	90	65	90	70	90	..	15
21......	..	..	..	..	..	45	30	40	85	90	60	90	70	90	..	15
22......	..	..	..	..	..	80	20	40	85	90	80	90	70	90	..	25
23......	..	..	..	..	..	80	20	60	85	90	85	90	70	90	..	25
24......	..	..	..	..	..	65	20	60	70	90	85	90	70	90	..	25
25......	..	..	..	..	..	65	..	50	70	90	80	90	75	90	..	30
26......	..	..	..	..	..	65	..	50	70	80	80	90	75	70	..	30
27......	..	..	..	..	..	65	..	30	50	80	80	90	70	70	.	30
28......	..	..	..	..	..	75	..	30	60	90	85	90	70	70	20	30
29......	..	..	..	..	..	75	..	40	75	90	85	90	70	60	20	30
30......	..	..	..	..	..	..	..	40	75	90	85	90	70	60	20	40
31......	..	..	..	..	..	..	..	50	10	90	..	..	70	20	..	40

Total, 1880... ... 8,520,000,000 gallons.
Total, 1881.. 8,605,000,000 "

TABLE 11.

Existing Storage—Artificial and Natural.

(From Report of August 12, 1879.)

The reservoirs and lakes within the Croton basin, and now available for storage purposes, are as follows:

	Gallons.
Boyd's Corners Reservoir	2,727,000,000
Middle Branch Reservoir	4,004,000,000
Lake Mahopac	575,000,000
Lake Kirk	565,000,000
Lake Gleneida	165,000,000
Lake Gilead	380,000,000
Lake Waccabuc	200,000,000
Lake Tonetta	50,000,000
Barrett's Pond	170,000,000
China Pond	105,000,000
White Pond	100,000,000
Pine Pond	75,000,000
Long Pond	60,000,000
Peach Pond	230,000,000
Cross Pond	110,000,000
Haine's Pond	25,000,000
Total Gallons	9,541,000,000

TABLE 12.

(From Report of August 12, 1879.)

The following table, prepared from daily observations for several years by the Engineers of the Croton Bureau, shows the rain-fall and the average daily quantity of water running in the Croton river:

Year.	Rainfall at Boyd's Corners Reservoir.	Average Daily Flow of the Croton River at Croton Dam.	Percentage of Rain-fall Running in the Stream.
	Inches.	Gallons.	Per cent.
1866	51.77	440,705,558	51.
1867	50.77	541,318,397	65.
1868	50.33	600,524,194	74.
1869	48.36	456,575,841	58.
1870	44.63	347,935,318	47.
1871	48.94	357,175,341	45.
1872	40.74	307,208,408	49.
1873	43.87	444,236,877	67.
1874	42.37	427,638,306	63.
1875	43.66	425,021,738	59.
1876	40.68	367,872,936	56.
1877	46.03	346,503,178	45.
1878	54.14	462,854,308	52.

www.ingramcontent.com/pod-product-compliance
Lightning Source LLC
La Vergne TN
LVHW010618110826
845149LV00003B/969

9781418186982